sweeter
OFF THE VINE

FRUIT DESSERTS FOR EVERY SEASON

YOSSY AREFI

TEN SPEED PRESS
Berkeley

CONTENTS

INTRODUCTION 1

SPRING

HERBS 11
chamomile honey panna cotta 12 | fresh mint
ice cream with cacao nibs 15 | lemon verbena
olive oil cake 16

RHUBARB 19
rhubarb and rose galettes 20 | rhubarb
semifreddo 24 | roasted rhubarb pavlova 27
| rhubarb and rye upside-down cake 31

STRAWBERRIES 35
the simplest strawberry tart 36 | strawberry
ice cream sandwiches with cacao nib poppy
seed wafers 39 | pistachio pound cake with
strawberries in lavender sugar 43 | strawberry
and campari paletas 47

CHERRIES 49
cherry and chocolate turnovers 50
| cherry and rhubarb slab pie 53 | spiked
cherry sorbet 55 | cherry and poppy seed
yogurt cake 59

SUMMER

APRICOTS 63
apricot and berry galette with saffron sugar 64
| small-batch apricot jam 67 | roasted apricot
and buttermilk sherbet 68

MIXED BERRIES 71
blueberry skillet cobbler with whole wheat
biscuits 72 | crème fraîche and blueberry ice
cream 75 | currant and gooseberry buckle 76
| blackberry and sage cream puffs 81 | black
fruit tart 85

MELONS 87
cantaloupe and mint yogurt pops 88
| watermelon granita with chile and lime 91

STONE FRUITS 95
nectarine and blackberry pie bars 96 | wine-
soaked peaches with lemon verbena 99 | spelt
shortcakes with roasted stone fruit 100 | plum
pie with hazelnut crumb 104

RASPBERRIES 107
coconut cream fool with raspberries 108
| chocolate celebration cake with fresh
raspberry buttercream 111 | raspberry sorbet
with pink peppercorns 116

FIGS 119
wine-roasted figs with whipped honeyed
ricotta 120 | soft chocolate and fig cake 123

FALL

GRAPES 127

concord grape pie with rye crust 128 | concord grape and plum butter 132

PERSIMMONS AND POMEGRANATES 137

jeweled pavlovas with cranberry curd 138 | persimmon sorbet with ginger and vanilla 142

APPLES 145

marie-danielle's apple tart 146 | caramelized apple fritters 151 | campfire crisp 155

PEARS 157

a pear-packed chestnut cake 158 | pear pie with crème fraîche caramel 161

QUINCE 165

ginger quince upside-down cake 166 | quince and pistachio frangipane tartlets 170

SQUASH AND PUMPKINS 173

butternut squash tea cake 174 | caramel-swirled roasted squash ice cream 179 | winter luxury pumpkin pie 180

WINTER

CRANBERRIES 185

cranberry bread pudding 186 | cornmeal and ricotta cake with cranberries 189 | cranberry and pear pandowdy 190

CITRUS 193

chocolate sesame tart with grapefruit 194 | blood orange old-fashioned donuts 197 | quick marmalade with blood oranges and meyer lemons 201 | tangerine cream pie 205 | grapefruit and meyer lemon bundt cake 208 | preserved lemon ice cream 212 | rangpur lime bars with saffron 215 | gingery lime posset 216 | citrus almond thumbprints with summer jam 219

DATES 221

sticky toffee pudding with cranberries 222 | browned-butter date blondies 225

YEAR-ROUND ESSENTIALS 227

all-butter pie crust 228 | crème fraîche 229 | crème fraîche caramel sauce 229 | crisp topping 230 | pastry cream 230 | spelt quick puff pastry 231 | sweet tart shell three ways: all-purpose, buckwheat, chocolate 232 | vanilla extract 235 | vanilla sugar 235

SEASONAL LARDER

poached quince 237 | preserved lemons 237 | roasted winter squash puree 238 | spiced rhubarb compote 240 | unsweetened cranberry juice 240

SOURCES 241 | ABOUT THE AUTHOR 242 | ACKNOWLEDGMENTS 243 | INDEX 244

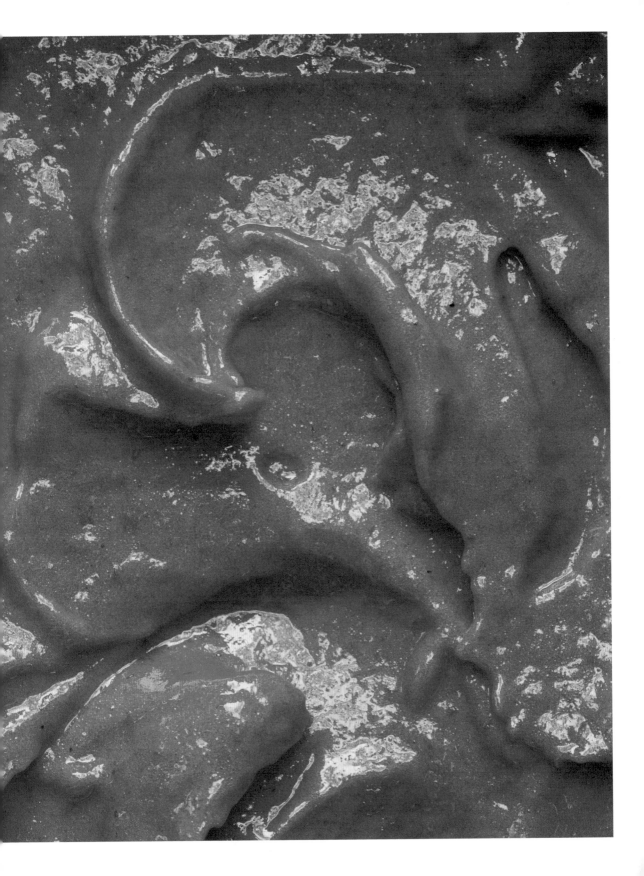

INTRODUCTION

Blackberries grow like weeds in the Pacific Northwest, and when I was a kid, my family picked the blackberries from the bushes behind an elementary school near our house every summer. My parents taught my brother and me to only pick the berries that slid easily from their stems to collect in our little plastic containers, and I'm pretty sure we ate all of the berries that we picked, staining our fingers and faces while leaving the majority of the actual collecting to the adults. When we got home, my mom would make a simple jam in our largest pot, with just blackberries and sugar.

My parents also loved to garden, and when we moved into a house with a yard, my dad built garden beds out of old railroad ties and filled them with fruit and vegetable plants. My mom planted an entire bed full of raspberry canes that looked like dried-up sticks; when they grew up tall and strong, they produced the most gorgeous berries. We picked them by the fistful every July and we turned our harvest into preserves and pies—and snacks, of course. I would stand in the kitchen and help my mom fill pies with mounds of fresh berries, sugar, and a bit of spice; we rarely measured, but the results were always delicious. She would bake up little scraps of pie crust sprinkled with cinnamon and sugar for me to snack on while the pies took what seemed like an eternity to cool on the counter.

The kitchen in our home was always busy and warm, and my dad cooked just as often, mostly savory dishes from his homeland of Iran. He introduced me to the flavors of Middle Eastern cooking that have become so comforting to me as an adult. But maybe more importantly, his cooking taught me how important it is to balance flavors in both sweet and savory food. In Iranian cooking, rich meat stews are tempered with cool, tart yogurt mixed with cucumbers and mint, and all sorts of pickled vegetables. Bitter tea is served with sweet dates and saffron candy.

When I moved to New York from Seattle, I thought I might go to culinary school to hone my home-cooking skills into professional ones, but after graduating college with a mountain of debt, taking on more to go to culinary school seemed like the wrong choice. Instead, I decided to get a job at a restaurant and figure out a way to get myself into the kitchen. I quickly found myself a job as a reservationist for a busy chain of teahouses, where I spent most of my time consoling frustrated customers who couldn't get the brunch reservation they wanted. It wasn't exactly the professional restaurant experience I was looking for.

I still baked at home for fun and leisure, and every once in a while I'd bring in the treats I made to share with my coworkers and boss. When a position in the bakery of the restaurant opened up, I convinced my boss that I could handle the kitchen (anything was better than answering the phone all day!) and pick up the skills I needed on the job. He gave me a chance.

That chance turned into many years of apron- and clog-clad early mornings making scones and icing cakes, and of coming home from work smelling sweet and floury. I had burns all over my arms from the broken oven doors that swung closed unexpectedly, but I was strong from lugging around fifty-pound bags of sugar and cases of butter. I learned how to make the best buttery pie crusts and tall, frosting-covered layer cakes. I loved the work. Sometimes I miss those early morning walks across a quiet Central Park to bake hundreds of scones before the city even woke up. There was magic in those hours, and even though I don't work as a baker anymore, I have returned to baking at home for fun, and I share it all on my blog, *Apt. 2B Baking Co.,* which celebrates seasonal desserts and preserves.

Although my current life in Brooklyn involves a "garden" of a few potted tomato plants and herbs on my fire escape, I make sure to embrace the seasons at my local farmers' market. I'm always looking for new, interesting dishes to cook and bake, but what I love most is reflecting seasonality through the ingredients I use, all while keeping the idea of balanced flavors in mind. I eagerly anticipate rhubarb in the spring, berries and stone fruit in the summer, apples and squash in the fall, and glorious citrus to brighten up cold East Coast winters. Then I celebrate the seasons' finest produce by tucking it into pies, cakes, and whatever else I can dream up and I also preserve the season with my own homemade jams. This book is filled with just those types of recipes.

We start in the spring, when everything is fresh and new. Fruit is slow to emerge, but there is plenty to do with strawberries and rhubarb. The bright flavors of spring's first green herbs are perfect for infusing into ice cream and panna cotta. In the summer, the variety and abundance of fruit can be almost overwhelming; in that section of the book, you will find pages of baked desserts, as well as cooling treats like granitas and sorbets, and jams to save the season. Fall highlights crisp apples and pears topped with oaty crumble and tucked into tarts. Musky Concord grapes will be turned into pie and roasted squash spun into ice cream or folded into nutty cake batter. In the winter, we move to warm, comforting recipes that will keep homes and bellies warm, and sunny citrus recipes that can brighten up the darkest January days.

This collection of recipes was written with peak-season fruit in mind, but some recipes straddle the seasons as spring turns to summer, summer to fall, and so on. So while this book is organized seasonally, it's best to think of the year as a continuum. Some years we are lucky and there are fresh figs at the market while the berries are still flourishing and the first grapes of fall are being pulled from their vines. Raspberries hit their peak at the height of summer, but often reappear in fall for a brief moment, perfectly timed to combine with the first tart red cranberries. Apples are plucked from their branches starting in late summer, but storage apples are available year-round. While winter is prime citrus season, when we have the biggest variety of lemons, oranges, and grapefruits, you will still find citrus zest and juice in recipes throughout the book. We are lucky in New York to have beautiful and bountiful farmers' markets, and I do my best to source my produce from local farmers. I encourage you to keep a close eye on what is available at the markets where you live and do the same.

The recipes in this book range from simple, five-ingredient affairs to more complex and involved baking endeavors like laminated pastry dough and composed tarts. My hope is that you'll find something that's just your speed, and that these recipes show the wide range of desserts you can make that highlight fresh, seasonal fruit all year. At the end of the book, you'll find a section full of basic recipes like oaty crisp topping, buttery pie crusts made with both whole grain and all purpose flours, pastry cream, and homemade vanilla extract and crème fraîche, among others. These recipes serve as the basis of many recipes throughout the book, and once you get the hang of them, I hope you'll feel free to freestyle some fruit desserts of your own.

spring

Spring begins not with a bang but a whisper: delicate green shoots begin to sprout up toward the sun, and herbs and flowers become plentiful. Mint pops up in its many varieties, from chocolate to pineapple to the delicately flavored Persian mint that threatens to take over my parents' garden every spring. Dormant lemon verbena plants begin to sprout their delicately flavored leaves and lavender buds open and release their delicious scent. Not far behind is rhubarb (technically a vegetable), which pops up in several varieties, some mostly green with red ends and some red to the core. Its stalks are tart and bracing, just begging to be roasted with a bit of sweetener and used in cakes, tarts, frozen desserts, and more. Soon strawberries, the first real fruit of the season, arrive. Tiny and best served raw, the first strawberries of the season are deep red all of the way through and juicy enough to stain your fingers. Finally, as spring nears its end, cherries appear. My home state of Washington is famous for its abundant cherries, with varieties from sweet Bings and Rainiers to the elusive sour cherries that are only around for a couple of weeks each year and are perfect for baking.

HERBS

THE FIRST FLAVORS OF SPRING ARE DELICATE
AND BRIGHT AS IF TO WARM UP OUR PALETTES
FOR THE BOUNTY TO COME LATER IN THE SEASON.
CHAMOMILE FLOWERS ARE MOST COMMONLY
DRIED AND USED FOR TEA, BUT THE FRESH FLOWERS
PAIR WELL WITH MILD-FLAVORED SPRING HONEYS.
MINT GROWS IN SEEMINGLY ENDLESS VARIETIES,
SOME WILD AND STRONG, AND SOME WITH
NAMES THAT SUGGEST HINTS OF OTHER FLAVORS
LIKE ORANGE AND CHOCOLATE. LEMON VERBENA
IS MY MOM'S FAVORITE HERB (MINE, TOO) AND
SHE GROWS A GIANT AMOUNT OF IT IN HER
GARDEN EVERY YEAR. AT THE END OF THE SEASON,
SHE CUTS LONG STEMS AND HANGS THEM TO
DRY IN BUNDLES IN THE GARAGE. THEN MY DAD
MAKES TEA FROM THE DRIED LEAVES ALL WINTER.

CHAMOMILE HONEY PANNA COTTA

| MAKES SIX 6-OUNCE PANNA COTTAS

With white petals surrounding their yellow centers, chamomile flowers look a lot like little daisies. In these sweet, milky custards, chamomile and honey are a natural pair—both of them floral and sweet. Top each panna cotta with coarsely chopped pistachios and a sprinkle of bee pollen for a vibrant and elegant dessert.

2 cups (480ml) heavy cream

½ cup (20g) fresh chamomile flowers, stems and leaves removed, or 2 chamomile tea bags

1 cup (240ml) whole milk

1 (¼-ounce/7g) envelope unflavored powdered gelatin

¼ cup (60ml) mild-flavored honey, like clover or wildflower

½ teaspoon vanilla extract (page 235)

Pinch salt

½ cup (65g) chopped pistachios, to serve

2 tablespoons bee pollen, to serve (optional)

Lightly grease six 6-ounce ramekins with a paper towel dipped in a bit of canola or grapeseed oil. Heat the cream in a saucepan set over medium heat until just barely simmering. Add the chamomile flowers (or tea bags), turn off the heat, and let steep for 20 minutes. Strain the cream through a fine-mesh sieve into a clean bowl and reserve.

Pour the milk into a clean saucepan and sprinkle the gelatin evenly over the top, but do not stir. Let the gelatin soften until the grains look wet and like they are beginning to dissolve, about 5 minutes. After the gelatin has bloomed, warm the milk and gelatin over very low heat, whisking occasionally, until the gelatin dissolves, 3 to 5 minutes. Be careful not to let the mixture bubble or simmer, which will inhibit the gelatin's ability to set.

Whisk in the honey, vanilla, and salt. Add the chamomile infused cream and whisk to combine. Divide the mixture among the ramekins and chill them in the refrigerator until set, at least 4 hours and up to overnight. If you are going to leave them overnight, cover each ramekin with plastic wrap.

To unmold the panna cottas, run a thin knife around the top edge of each ramekin to release the sides, and invert it onto a plate; you may have to shake the ramekin gently to get the panna cotta to release onto the plate. Top each panna cotta with a sprinkle of chopped pistachios and a dusting of bee pollen. Alternatively, serve the panna cottas in their ramekins with the garnishes.

FRESH MINT ICE CREAM WITH CACAO NIBS

| MAKES ABOUT 1 QUART (900G)

This fresh-tasting ice cream is packed with pleasantly crunchy and slightly bitter cacao nibs, like mint chocolate chip all grown up. I don't add any food coloring to this recipe, but I won't judge if you feel compelled to add a drop or two of green to the custard just before churning. Sometimes that tint really does make the mint flavor shine. Try making this ice cream with chocolate mint or pineapple mint for a bit of extra flavor.

1 cup loosely packed (15g) fresh mint leaves, coarsely chopped

4 large egg yolks

2 cups (480ml) heavy cream

1 cup (240ml) whole milk

⅔ cup (135g) granulated sugar

2 tablespoons Crème Fraîche (page 229)

¼ cup (40g) cacao nibs

Whisk the egg yolks together in a glass or stainless steel bowl; set aside.

Combine the cream, milk, sugar, and salt in a medium saucepan. Heat over medium heat, stirring occasionally, until the mixture begins to bubble around the edges, about 5 minutes. Ladle about 1 cup of the cream mixture into the egg yolks and whisk vigorously to temper. Pour the egg and cream mixture back into the pot and whisk well to combine.

Cook the mixture on medium low heat, stirring constantly with a rubber spatula and being careful not to let it boil, until the mixture thickens enough to coat the back of a spoon, about 7 minutes. Remove from the heat and whisk in the crème fraîche, then the mint leaves. Allow the mixture to cool to room temperature, then cover and refrigerate to chill completely, at least 4 hours and up to overnight. The longer the mint steeps, the stronger the mint flavor will be.

Just before churning, strain the custard through a fine-mesh sieve and press gently on the mint leaves to extract all of the liquid. Freeze in an ice cream machine according to the manufacturer's instructions, adding the cacao nibs in the last minute of churning. Transfer the ice cream to a freezer-safe container, cover and freeze until firm, about 4 hours or overnight. Keeps for four days.

LEMON VERBENA OLIVE OIL CAKE

| MAKES ONE 9-INCH CAKE

As evidenced by its name, lemon verbena has a citrusy flavor that pairs exceptionally well with lemon zest and fruity olive oil in this cake. Try dusting the cooled cake with a bit of confectioners' sugar to elevate its pleasantly humble appearance or serve it with sliced strawberries macerated with a pinch of sugar later in the season when strawberries are at their peak.

1 cup (200g) granulated sugar

¼ cup loosely packed fresh lemon verbena leaves (about 20)

1¾ cups (225g) all purpose flour

1 teaspoon baking powder

½ teaspoon baking soda

¼ teaspoon salt

¾ cup (175ml) fruity olive oil

¼ cup (55g) unsalted butter, melted and cooled

1 teaspoon lemon zest

4 large eggs, at room temperature

1 cup (240ml) whole-milk kefir or buttermilk, at room temperature

2 tablespoons confectioners' sugar, to finish

Position a rack in the center of the oven and preheat to 350°F (180°C). Butter a 9-inch cake pan at least 2 inches tall, line it with parchment paper, and butter that, too. Dust the pan and paper with flour.

Combine the sugar and lemon verbena in the bowl of a food processor fitted with a steel blade or in a mortar. Pulse or grind the sugar and lemon verbena until the leaves are finely ground and the sugar is fragrant.

Whisk the flour, baking powder, baking soda, and salt together in a small bowl.

In a separate bowl, whisk the lemon verbena sugar, olive oil, melted butter, and lemon zest together. Add the eggs and whisk for 30 more seconds. Whisk in the kefir, then use a rubber spatula to fold in the dry ingredients, mixing until combined and smooth.

Pour the batter into the prepared pan, tap it gently on the counter to release any air bubbles, and bake until the cake is puffed and golden and a cake tester inserted into the center comes out clean, 40 to 45 minutes. Cool the cake in the pan on a rack for 20 minutes, then remove the cake from the pan to cool completely. Dust the cooled cake with a bit of confectioners' sugar just before serving, if you like. This cake will keep in an airtight container at room temperature for up to three days.

RHUBARB

MY FRIEND CAMILLE LIVES IN OREGON AND
GROWS THE PRETTIEST RHUBARB I'VE EVER SEEN.
IT IS DEEPLY CRIMSON ALL THE WAY TO THE CORE,
UNLIKE THE MOSTLY GREEN RHUBARB THAT IS
GROWN IN NEW YORK. KNOWING HOW MUCH
I LOVE THE STUFF, CAMILLE ONCE BROUGHT ME
A DUFFLE BAG FULL OF BRIGHT RED STALKS FROM
HER GARDEN. I CAN ONLY IMAGINE WHAT THE
AIRLINE THOUGHT OF THAT CARRY ON. RHUBARB
COMES IN MANY VARIETIES THAT RANGE FROM
DEEP RED TO MOSTLY GREEN. I PREFER THE MORE
BRIGHTLY HUED VARIETIES FOR BAKING BECAUSE
THEIR BEAUTIFUL COLOR POPS, BUT THE GOOD
NEWS IS THAT MOST RHUBARB VARIETIES TASTE
VERY SIMILAR. JUST MAKE SURE TO REMOVE ANY
LEAVES FROM THE STALKS BEFORE COOKING,
AS THEY ARE POISONOUS.

RHUBARB AND ROSE GALETTES

| MAKES 8 INDIVIDUAL GALETTES

Rhubarb galettes are almost always my first baking project each spring because they combine my favorite ingredient (rhubarb) and with my favorite preparation, galettes. This style of tart is meant to be rustic and loose, so don't worry if they don't look totally perfect as they go into the oven; it just adds to their charm. Finish each tart with a spoonful of rose water–infused cream.

GALETTES

1 recipe (720g) Spelt Pie Crust (see spelt variation on All-Butter Pie Crust, page 228) dough, shaped into squares rather than disks before wrapping and chilling

1 pound (450g) rhubarb stalks, leaves removed

1 vanilla bean

½ teaspoon lemon zest

¾ cup (150g) granulated sugar

2 tablespoons all purpose flour

Pinch salt

2 tablespoons lemon juice

2 teaspoons rose water

1 large egg lightly beaten, for egg wash

2 tablespoons turbinado sugar

ROSE CREAM

1 cup (240ml) heavy cream

1 tablespoon rose water

2 teaspoons sugar

To make the galettes: Line two baking sheets with parchment paper. Slice the rhubarb stalks lengthwise in half, then slice each half into roughly ½ by 3-inch lengths to make long, skinny batons. Use the tip of a knife to slice the vanilla bean in half lengthwise and scrape out the seeds reserve the pod for another use.

In a large bowl, use your fingers to rub the vanilla seeds and lemon zest into the sugar, then add the flour and salt. Add the rhubarb batons to the bowl along with the lemon juice and rose water. Toss the rhubarb with the sugar and flour mixture to coat.

Remove one square of the pie dough from the refrigerator and cut it into quarters. On a lightly floured surface, roll each dough quarter into a 4 by 5-inch rectangle between ⅛ to ¼-inch thick. Transfer the four rectangles of dough to one of the prepared baking sheets. Arrange one-eighth of the rhubarb batons in a single, slightly overlapping layer on each piece of dough, leaving a generous ½-inch border around all sides. Fold the excess dough up and over the rhubarb and press the corner seams gently with your fingers to seal. Put the baking sheet in the freezer and repeat with the remaining dough and rhubarb. Place that baking sheet in the freezer, too, and freeze until the dough is very firm, about 15 minutes. Save any rhubarb juices that remain in the bottom of the bowl.

CONTINUED

RHUBARB AND ROSE GALETTES, CONTINUED

While the galettes are chilling, position two racks in the center and lower third of the oven, and preheat to 425ºF (220ºC). When you are ready to bake the galettes, brush the edges of each galette with the egg wash and sprinkle with turbinado sugar. Top the rhubarb in each galette with a spoonful of the reserved rhubarb juices. Bake the galettes, rotating the pans from top to bottom and front to back halfway through baking, until they are deep golden brown and crisp, 30 to 40 minutes.

To make the rose cream: Whip the cream with the rose water and sugar until soft peaks form. Store the cream in the refrigerator until ready to serve. Let the tarts cool slightly before serving. Top each tart with a spoonful of cream and serve immediately.

RHUBARB SEMIFREDDO

| SERVES 8-10

Semifreddo is an Italian style frozen dessert, served in thick slices rather than scoops and has the texture of frozen mousse. This version, packed with roasted rhubarb, is creamy, light, and tart. If you'd like to dress it up, make the Spiced Rhubarb Compote (page 240) and serve each slice with a little spoonful along with the cream and pistachios.

12 ounces (340g) rhubarb stalks, leaves removed

1 cup (200g) sugar

¼ teaspoon salt

4 large eggs

1½ cups (355ml) heavy cream

½ cup (60g) chopped pistachios, to serve (optional)

Lightly sweetened whipped cream, to serve (optional)

Spiced Rhubarb Compote, to serve (page 240; optional)

Position a rack in the center of the oven and preheat to 375ºF (190ºC). Line a 9 by 5 by 3-inch loaf pan with plastic wrap, making sure there are at least 3 inches of overhang on each side.

To roast the rhubarb: Slice the rhubarb stalks into 2-inch pieces and put them in a baking dish large enough to hold them in a single layer. Sprinkle ¾ cup of the sugar and the salt over the top and toss gently to combine. Bake for about 15 minutes, or until the rhubarb is soft and juicy. Let the rhubarb cool slightly, then transfer to a food processor or blender and blend until smooth. You should have about 2 cups of rhubarb puree. Refrigerate while you prepare the rest of the ingredients.

Whip the eggs with an electric mixer on high speed with the remaining ¼ cup sugar until the eggs are light in color and have nearly tripled in volume, about 7 minutes. In a separate bowl, with clean beaters, whip the cream to soft peaks.

Whisk the chilled rhubarb puree into the eggs until well combined. Don't worry if the eggs lose some volume. Fold in the whipped cream, then spread the mixture in the prepared pan, and smooth the surface. Fold the plastic wrap over the top to cover, pressing it against the surface to seal. Freeze until completely firm, at least 6 hours or overnight.

To serve: unwrap the plastic from the top of the pan, invert the semifreddo onto a platter, and remove the remaining plastic. Serve thick slices of semifreddo with a bit of whipped cream and chopped pistachios or a spoonful of Spiced Rhubarb Compote (page 240). Extra semifreddo can be stored in the freezer, wrapped tightly in plastic wrap, for up to five days.

ROASTED RHUBARB PAVLOVA

| MAKES ONE 8-INCH PAVLOVA

MERINGUE

1 cup (200g) superfine sugar

1½ teaspoons cornstarch

4 large egg whites

¼ teaspoon salt

⅛ teaspoon cream of tartar

1 teaspoon vanilla extract (page 235)

1 teaspoon white vinegar

RHUBARB

12 ounces (340g) rhubarb stalks, leaves removed

1 vanilla bean

⅓ cup (67g) granulated sugar

Pinch salt

Juice of ½ lemon (about 4 teaspoons)

TO SERVE

1 cup (240ml) heavy cream

1 tablespoon granulated sugar

3 tablespoons pomegranate molasses

Pavlova is a traditional Australian dessert comprised of three main components: a crisp and chewy meringue base, fruit, and cream. This particular recipe combines vanilla-infused roasted rhubarb with whipped cream and is topped with pomegranate molasses. Pomegranate molasses is a staple in many Middle Eastern cuisines and is sweet, tart, and tangy, making it a perfect pairing with rhubarb. It can be found at any Middle Eastern market, and often times at natural foods stores.

Position a rack in the center of the oven and preheat to 225ºF (110ºC). Trace an 8-inch circle onto a piece of parchment paper and flip the paper upside down on a baking sheet.

To make the meringue: Stir the cornstarch and sugar together in a small bowl. In the bowl of a stand mixer fitted with the whisk attachment or with a handheld electric mixer in a large bowl, beat the egg whites, salt, and cream of tartar on medium high speed until soft peaks form. Turn the mixer up to high and with the mixer running, slowly add the sugar mixture about one tablespoon at a time and whip until the egg whites are stiff and glossy, about 7 minutes. Add the vanilla and vinegar and mix for 30 more seconds.

Dollop the meringue onto the prepared baking sheet and use an offset spatula to spread it evenly to the edges of the traced circle. Make a shallow (½-inch) indent in the center of the meringue leaving a 1-inch border around the edges; this will hold the rhubarb and whipped cream. Bake the meringue for 1 to 1½ hours or until the outside looks dry and slightly creamy in color. Turn off the oven and prop the door ajar with a wooden spoon. Let the meringue cool completely in the oven. It should feel firm and crackly when you press it, but will be soft and marshmallowy in the center. When cooled, you should be able to gently peel it off of the parchment paper and place it on a serving platter

CONTINUED

or cake stand. The meringue can be prepared a day in advance and stored in an airtight container.

To roast the rhubarb: Preheat the oven to 375º (190ºC). Cut the rhubarb stalks into 3-inch lengths. Use the tip of a knife to split the vanilla bean lengthwise and scrape out the seeds. In a baking dish large enough to hold the rhubarb in a single layer, toss the cut rhubarb with the vanilla bean seeds, sugar, salt, and lemon juice; tuck the vanilla bean pod in among the rhubarb. Bake until the rhubarb is soft and juicy but not falling apart, 20 to 25 minutes. Let cool to room temperature, then remove the vanilla bean pod, rinse it off, and save it for another use.

To assemble: Whip the cream and sugar together to stiff peaks. Top the cooled meringue with the whipped cream, then the cooled roasted rhubarb pieces. Finish by drizzling with the pomegranate molasses and any rhubarb juices left in the baking pan. Slice into wedges and serve immediately.

RHUBARB AND RYE UPSIDE-DOWN CAKE

| MAKES ONE 9-INCH CAKE

RHUBARB TOPPING

1 pound (450g) rhubarb, leaves removed, cut into 2-inch (5cm) lengths

1 vanilla bean

¾ cup (150g) granulated sugar

¼ cup (55g) unsalted butter

1 teaspoon lemon zest

Pinch salt

CAKE

1 cup (125g) all purpose flour

1 cup (130g) rye flour

1 tablespoon baking powder

½ teaspoon baking soda

½ teaspoon salt

½ cup (115g) unsalted butter, softened

½ cup (100g) granulated sugar

2 large eggs, at room temperature

1 teaspoon vanilla extract (page 235)

1½ cups (355ml) buttermilk, at room temperature

TO SERVE

Lightly sweetened whipped cream or ice cream

An upside-down cake is a great way to highlight just about any fruit, but this springy version is especially nice. The cake batter is light, fluffy, and speckled with just enough rye flour to make it interesting. As the cake bakes, the tart rhubarb juices caramelize into a delicious sauce that soaks into the cake as it cooks. This is perfect with a little vanilla ice cream on the side.

Position a rack in the center of the oven and preheat to 375ºF (190ºC). Butter a 9-inch cake pan or springform pan, 3 inches tall, line it with parchment paper, and butter that too. Dust the pan and paper with flour.

To make the rhubarb topping: Use the tip of a knife to split the vanilla bean lengthwise and scrape out the seeds; reserve the pod for another use. Combine the sugar, butter, vanilla seeds, lemon zest, and salt in a skillet and set over medium low heat. Heat, stirring occasionally, until the sugar and butter begin to melt together, then add the rhubarb. Cook the rhubarb, turning it occasionally in the pan, until it is juicy, tender, and slightly caramelized but not falling apart, 6 to 8 minutes. Pour the rhubarb and its juices into the prepared pan and spread in an even layer. Set aside while you prepare the cake batter.

To make the cake: In a medium bowl, whisk the all purpose and rye flours, baking powder, baking soda, and salt together. In the bowl of a stand mixer fitted with the paddle attachment, cream the butter and sugar together at medium high speed until light and fluffy, about 5 minutes. Add the eggs, one at a time, mixing for 30 seconds after each addition. Add the vanilla. Use a rubber spatula to scrape down the sides and bottom of the bowl. Alternate adding the flour mixture and the buttermilk in three additions and mix until just combined. Carefully pour the batter over the rhubarb in the pan and smooth the top. Tap the pan gently on the counter to remove any air bubbles. If using a springform pan, set it on a baking sheet to catch any potential leakage.

CONTINUED

RHUBARB AND RYE UPSIDE-DOWN CAKE, CONTINUED

Bake the cake until the top is golden and a cake tester inserted into the center comes out clean, 30 to 35 minutes. Let the cake cool on a rack for 15 minutes, then carefully invert onto a serving platter. Remove the parchment paper and reposition any rhubarb that has stuck to the paper. Cut into wedges and serve warm with whipped cream or ice cream, if you like. This cake is best served the day that it's made.

STRAWBERRIES

STRAWBERRIES ARE AVAILABLE YEAR-ROUND IN MOST PARTS OF THE UNITED STATES, BUT THE BEST STRAWBERRIES POP UP AT FARMERS' MARKETS IN LATE MAY AND EARLY JUNE (FOR US EAST COASTERS, AT LEAST). STRAWBERRIES FROM THE FARMERS' MARKET ARE GENERALLY SMALLER AND DEEPER IN COLOR AND FLAVOR THAN SUPERMARKET STRAWBERRIES, BUT THEY ALSO TEND TO BE MORE DELICATE AND PERISHABLE, SO PLAN TO EAT THEM SOON AFTER YOU BRING THEM HOME. MY FAVORITE STRAWBERRY IS THE TINY, JEWEL-LIKE TRISTAR, A HYBRID VARIETY THAT IS HALF WILD AND ALL DELICIOUS.

THE SIMPLEST STRAWBERRY TART

| MAKES ONE 15 BY 6-INCH TART

I'm not one for hyperbole, especially when it comes to food, but this truly is the simplest strawberry tart, and it's more delicious than the sum of its parts. This tart is all about the contrasting textures of crisp crust, creamy mascarpone, and juicy strawberries, so make sure to assemble the tart right before you serve it so the crust doesn't get soggy.

½ recipe Rye Pie Crust (see rye variation on All-Butter Pie Crust, page 228)

1 large egg, lightly beaten for egg wash

1 pound (450g) small sweet strawberries

1 cup (225g) mascarpone

3 tablespoons Vanilla Sugar (page 235) or granulated sugar

3 tablespoons high-quality strawberry jam

Position a rack in the center of the oven and preheat to 400ºF (200ºC).

On a lightly floured piece of parchment paper, roll out the pie crust disk into an oval about 15 by 6 inches and just under ¼-inch thick. Use a paring knife or pastry cutter to trim any rough edges and move the parchment sheet and crust to a baking sheet. Dock the crust with a fork to prevent it from puffing up too much in the oven. Brush the surface of the crust from edge to edge with the egg wash. Bake the dough until it is deep golden brown, 25 to 30 minutes. Check on the crust halfway through baking and if any bubbles have appeared, use a spatula to press them flat. Cool the crust completely on the pan.

While the crust is cooling, combine the mascarpone and 2 tablespoons of the sugar. Hull the strawberries and slice them into ¼-inch slices.

Move the cooled pie crust to a serving platter or board and spread the mascarpone over the top in an even layer, dot with the jam, then arrange the sliced strawberries in a single, slightly overlapping layer in a decorative pattern. Sprinkle the tart with the remaining tablespoon of sugar (omit this final sprinkling if your strawberries are particularly sweet), slice, and serve immediately.

SEASONAL VARIATIONS: This combination of buttery crust and sweetened mascarpone would work with just about any fresh fruit. Later in the summer, blackberries, raspberries, or sliced peaches or nectarines would all be lovely with Small-Batch Apricot Jam (page 67) substituted for the strawberry.

STRAWBERRY ICE CREAM SANDWICHES WITH CACAO NIB POPPY SEED WAFERS

| MAKES ABOUT 18 SANDWICHES

STRAWBERRY ICE CREAM

1 pound (450g) strawberries halved

1 cup (200g) granulated sugar

4 large egg yolks

1 cup (240ml) whole milk

2 cups (480ml) heavy cream

¼ teaspoon salt

2 tablespoons Crème Fraîche (page 229)

2 tablespoons golden syrup or light corn syrup

WAFERS

1 cup (85g) old-fashioned oats

6 tablespoons (50g) buckwheat flour

2 tablespoons poppy seeds

1 tablespoon cacao nibs

1½ teaspoons baking powder

¼ teaspoon salt

½ cup (115g) unsalted butter, melted and cooled

1 cup (200g) granulated sugar

1 large egg, at room temperature

1 teaspoon vanilla extract (page 235)

The key to perfect ice cream sandwiches are the cookies. You want the kind of cookie that you can easily bite through, even when frozen, so that all of the ice cream inside doesn't squeeze out and end up all over your face (or your lap). These lacy cookies made from slightly bitter buckwheat flour, filled with crunchy poppy seeds and cacao nibs, fit that bill and they are naturally gluten free. The sweet roasted strawberry ice cream balances the bitter flavors nicely. This recipe makes quite a few ice cream sandwiches, but the cookies and ice cream are both individually delicious, and freeze well, so don't worry if you have leftovers.

Position a rack in the center of the oven and preheat to 375ºF (190ºC).

To make the strawberry ice cream: Toss the cut strawberries and 1/3 cup sugar on a baking sheet. Roast the berries until the juices start to caramelize, 15 to 20 minutes. Let the berries cool slightly then puree them in a blender or food processor until smooth. Set aside.

Whisk the egg yolks together in a glass or stainless steel bowl; set aside. Combine the milk, cream, remaining 2/3 cup of sugar, and salt in a medium saucepan. Heat over medium heat, stirring occasionally, until the mixture begins to bubble around the edges.

Ladle about 1 cup of the cream mixture into the egg yolks and whisk vigorously. Pour the egg and cream mixture back into the pan and whisk well to combine. Cook the mixture on medium low heat and cook, stirring constantly with a rubber spatula and being careful not to let it boil, until the mixture thickens enough to coat the back of a spoon, about 7 minutes.

CONTINUED

Turn off the heat and whisk in the crème fraîche, golden syrup, and roasted strawberry puree. Strain the mixture through a fine-mesh sieve and allow the custard to cool to room temperature, then refrigerate to chill completely, at least 4 hours or overnight.

Freeze in an ice cream machine according to manufacturer's instructions, then transfer the ice cream to a freezer-safe container. Cover and freeze until firm, about 4 hours or overnight.

To make the wafers: Position two racks in the center and upper third of the oven and preheat to 325ºF (165ºC). Line two baking sheets with parchment paper.

In a medium bowl, stir the flour, oats, poppy seeds, cacao nibs, baking powder, and salt together until well combined. In a separate bowl, use a rubber spatula to stir butter and sugar together. Add the egg and vanilla and stir until well combined. Add the dry ingredients all at once and stir until just combined.

Drop the batter by rounded teaspoons onto the prepared baking sheets at least 2 inches apart. The wafers will spread and flatten quite a bit as they bake. Bake the wafers, rotating the pans in the oven halfway through from top to bottom and front to back, until lacy and golden brown on the edges, 9 to 11 minutes. Let the wafers cool completely on the baking sheets, then carefully remove them from the parchment paper. Repeat until all of the batter is used.

To assemble: Remove the ice cream from the freezer about 10 minutes before you want to make the sandwiches, to soften slightly. Decide how many sandwiches you want to make, and select twice as many wafers. Flip half of the wafers over so their flat sides are up. Top each wafer with a small scoop of ice cream (a cookie scoop works great for this) and top the ice cream with another wafer, flat side down. Put the sandwiches on a parchment-lined baking sheet or plate and refreeze until they're firm, about 45 minutes. Either serve them immediately, or wrap them individually in plastic wrap and store for up to two days in the freezer.

PISTACHIO POUND CAKE WITH STRAWBERRIES IN LAVENDER SUGAR

| MAKES ONE 9 BY 5-INCH CAKE

PISTACHIO POUND CAKE

1 cup (130g) shelled pistachios

1½ cups (195g) all purpose flour

½ teaspoon baking powder

¾ teaspoon salt

¾ cup (175g) unsalted butter, softened

1¼ cups (250g) granulated sugar

3 large eggs, at room temperature

½ teaspoon vanilla extract (page 235)

¼ teaspoon almond extract

½ cup (120ml) whole milk, at room temperature

STRAWBERRIES

1½ pounds (675g) strawberries

¼ cup (50g) granulated sugar, or less if your berries are particularly sweet

½ teaspoon organic lavender buds

½ vanilla bean, split lengthwise and seeds scraped from the pod

TO SERVE

Lightly sweetened whipped cream

The rich flavor and beautiful color of pistachios makes them the perfect addition to this classic pound cake. The strawberries here are sweetened with just a bit of lavender-infused sugar, which imparts a subtle and light floral flavor, perfect for spring. I like to serve this cake in thick slices with generous spoonfuls of juicy berries and a dollop of whipped cream, like strawberry shortcake, but better. Culinary grade lavender is available at many spice shops, farmers' markets, and online, but a tablespoon or so of chopped mint or basil leaves is a fine substitute.

Position a rack in the center of the oven, preheat to 325ºF (165ºC). Grease and flour a 9 by 5 by 3-inch loaf pan.

To make the cake: Grind the pistachios in a food processor just until they resemble flour. Be careful to not grind them into pistachio butter, though that would be delicious. Add the flour, baking powder, and salt to the bowl of the food processor. Pulse until combined.

In the bowl of a stand mixer fitted with the paddle attachment, or in a large bowl with an electric mixer, beat the butter on medium high speed until smooth, then, with the mixer still running, slowly stream in the sugar. Cream the butter and sugar together until very light and fluffy, about 5 minutes. Add the eggs one at a time, beating for 30 seconds after each addition. Occasionally stop the mixer and scrape down the sides of the bowl to ensure even mixing. Add the vanilla and almond extracts.

With the mixer on low speed, alternate adding the flour mixture and the milk to the batter in three additions, mixing until just combined. Finish mixing the batter by hand with a rubber spatula. Make sure to scrape the bottom and sides of the bowl to ensure even mixing.

CONTINUED

PISTACHIO POUND CAKE WITH STRAWBERRIES IN LAVENDER SUGAR, CONTINUED

Pour the batter into the prepared pan, smooth the top, and bake until the cake is golden brown and a toothpick inserted into the center comes out clean, 45 to 55 minutes. Cool for 15 minutes in the pan, then remove the cake to a rack to cool completely.

To make the strawberries: Combine the sugar, lavender, and vanilla seeds in a mortar and grind with a pestle until the lavender is broken up into fine bits and the sugar is fragrant. Alternately, this can be done in a food processor. Hull and slice the strawberries in half if they are small, in quarters if they are larger; combine the sliced strawberries and sugar in a bowl and stir gently. Let the berries macerate for at least 15 minutes at room temperature before serving.

To serve: Slice the cooled cake into thick pieces and top each slice with a generous spoonful of berries and their juices. Top with whipped cream. Extra cake keeps in an airtight container at room temperature for three days.

STRAWBERRY AND CAMPARI PALETAS

| MAKES 6 TO 12 PALETAS, DEPENDING ON THE SIZE OF THE MOLDS

Paletas are ice pops made from fresh fruit; this version combines sweet strawberries and bitter, herbaceous Campari for a grown-up frozen treat. Be careful not to get too carried away with the Campari—too much booze and these pops won't freeze. For a refreshing cocktail, try serving the paletas dipped in a glass of Prosecco: trust me, it's delicious.

1 pound (450g) strawberries

5 tablespoons (60g) granulated sugar

¼ cup (60ml) Campari

Juice of ½ lemon (about 4 teaspoons)

Pinch salt

Hull the strawberries and slice them in half. Add them, along with the rest of the ingredients, to a blender or food processor and blend until smooth. Taste the mixture and adjust the level of sweetness if necessary by adding more sugar, one teaspoon at time. Strain through a fine-mesh sieve and pour into frozen pop molds. Freeze the pops until completely firm, at least 6 hours or overnight.

CHERRIES

WHEN SHOPPING FOR CHERRIES, LOOK FOR PLUMP FRUIT WITH SMOOTH SKINS AND GREEN STEMS. CHERRIES WITH DARK STEMS AND BROWN SPOTS ARE PAST THEIR PRIME AND SHOULD BE AVOIDED. DEEP RED CHERRY VARIETIES, LIKE BING, CHELAN, AND LAMBERT, AND SOUR VARIETIES LIKE MORELLO AND MONTGOMERY, ARE THE BEST FOR BAKING. LIGHTER COLORED CHERRIES, SUCH AS RAINIER OR QUEEN ANNE, ARE ALSO DELICIOUS, BUT ARE BEST EATEN STRAIGHT FRESH, STRAIGHT OUT OF HAND. A CHERRY PITTING TIP: PIT CHERRIES OVER YOUR KITCHEN SINK (OR OUTSIDE) TO AVOID STAINING YOUR COUNTERTOPS AND WALLS WITH RED SPLATTERS.

CHERRY AND CHOCOLATE TURNOVERS

| MAKES 6 TURNOVERS

I used to turn up my nose at the combination of fruit and chocolate, but the pairing of sweet cherries and bittersweet chocolate in this homemade buttery pastry made me a convert. Make sure to bake these until they are truly deep golden brown. The sign of a great turnover is a lap full of flaky golden crumbs when you finish eating it, so make sure to give your guests an extra napkin when you serve these.

⅓ recipe (450g) Spelt Quick Puff Pastry (page 231)

10 ounces (280g) sweet cherries, pitted

1 tablespoon lemon juice

2 tablespoons granulated sugar

½ teaspoon vanilla extract (page 235)

1 teaspoon cornstarch

1 tablespoon water

1 large egg, lightly beaten for egg wash

6 tablespoons (60g) chopped bittersweet chocolate

2 teaspoons turbinado sugar

1 teaspoon flaky sea salt

Combine the cherries, lemon juice, sugar, and vanilla in a wide skillet. Cook over medium high heat until the cherries soften and they begin to release their juices and simmer, about 5 minutes. Whisk the cornstarch and water together in a small bowl and quickly stir it into the cherry juices. Cook for one more minute, stirring constantly. The juices will thicken. Set aside to cool.

Line a baking sheet with parchment paper. On a lightly floured surface, roll the pastry into a rectangle about 10 by 15 inches. Trim the edges so they are straight and even, then cut the rectangle into six, 5-inch squares. Place a generous spoonful of the cooled cherry mixture in the center of each turnover and top with a tablespoon of chopped chocolate. Take care to not overfill the turnovers or the edges will not seal properly and the filling will spill out onto the baking sheet. Brush the edges of the dough with the egg wash and fold each square in half diagonally to form a triangle. Press the edges together with a fork to seal well. Transfer the turnovers to the prepared baking sheet and freeze for 15 minutes or until the pastry is very firm.

Meanwhile, position a rack in the center of the oven and preheat to 425ºF (220ºC). When you are ready to bake, brush the turnovers with the remaining beaten egg and sprinkle with turbinado sugar and a few grains of flaky sea salt. Use the tip of a knife to cut a small slit into the top of each turnover. Bake the turnovers until they are deep golden brown, 20 to 25 minutes. Let cool slightly before serving. These turnovers are best served warm, the day they are baked, but will keep at room temperature for two days.

CHERRY AND RHUBARB SLAB PIE

| MAKES ONE 18 BY 13-INCH PIE

My ideal cherry pie is chock full of sour cherries, but their short season and limited availability sometimes makes them difficult to find. In this slab pie, I combined early season sweet cherries with rhubarb to mimic the lovely sweet-and-tart flavor of sour cherries. Slab pie is pie for a crowd, so you'll need a half sheet pan for this recipe, which is a bit bigger than a traditional jelly roll pan.

2 recipes (1440g) All-Butter Pie Crust (page 228), each batch shaped into a single rectangle rather than 2 disks.

1 vanilla bean

1 cup (200g) granulated sugar

¾ teaspoon orange zest

2 pounds (900g) rhubarb, leaves removed and stalks chopped into ½-inch pieces

1 pound (450g) sweet cherries, pitted, halved if large

¼ cup (32g) cornstarch

Pinch salt

Juice of 1 lemon (about 3 tablespoons)

1 large egg, lightly beaten, for egg wash

2 tablespoons turbinado sugar

Begin by rolling out one of the pieces of dough between two lightly floured sheets of parchment paper to a roughly 21 by 16-inch rectangle. It is a big piece of dough, so it will take a little muscle to roll out. The rectangle does not have to be perfectly shaped, but if the dough cracks or breaks, repair the breaks with a bit of dough pulled from the edges of the sheet. If at any time the dough seems very soft or sticky, slide it, along with the parchment paper, onto a baking sheet and stick the whole thing in the fridge for a couple of minutes. Remove the parchment paper and carefully fit the dough into an 18 by 13 by 1-inch baking sheet (half sheet pan). Press the dough into the corners and let the edges hang over the sides.

Roll out the remaining piece of dough between two floured pieces of parchment paper into a rectangle about 18 by 13 by 1-inches. Transfer the lined half sheet pan and the dough sheet to the refrigerator to chill while you prepare the rest of the pie.

To make the filling: Use the tip of a knife to split the vanilla bean lengthwise and scrape out the seeds; reserve the pod for another use. In a large bowl, combine the sugar, orange zest, and vanilla seeds. Use your fingers to rub the zest and vanilla seeds into the sugar until well distributed. Stir in the cornstarch and salt, then add the rhubarb, cherries, and lemon juice. Toss gently to combine. Add a bit more cornstarch (up to 1 tablespoon) if the cherries are particularly juicy.

CONTINUED

CHERRY AND RHUBARB SLAB PIE, CONTINUED

Remove the dough-lined pan from the fridge and spread the filling evenly over the top. Remove the parchment paper from the second dough sheet and place it on top of the filling. Fold the bottom edges up and over the top and press the edges of both crusts together to seal. Refrigerate the pie until the crust is firm, about 20 minutes.

Meanwhile, position a rack in the center of the oven and preheat to 400ºF (200ºC).

Brush the top crust with the egg wash and sprinkle the turbinado sugar over the top. Use a small knife to cut a few vents in the top crust, then bake the pie until it is deep golden brown and the juices are bubbling, 40 to 45 minutes. Cool the pie to room temperature before slicing and serving. This pie is best served the day it is baked, but it will keep for a couple of days wrapped in plastic wrap and refrigerated. The pastry will soften as the pie sits.

SEASONAL VARIATION: Substitute an equal amount of pitted sour cherries for the rhubarb and sweet cherries, if they are available.

SPIKED CHERRY SORBET

| MAKES ABOUT 3 CUPS (680G)

My boyfriend makes a mean Manhattan: boozy, balanced, and just slightly sweet. My favorite part is always the whiskey-soaked cherry at the bottom of the glass. This sorbet is like a giant bowl of those cherries. The alcohol in this recipe prevents the sorbet from freezing solid, so serve it straight from the freezer in chilled bowls, rather than scooped on cones.

1 pound (450g) pitted sweet cherries

¼ cup (60ml) water

½ cup (100g) granulated sugar

1 tablespoon lemon juice

2 tablespoons rye whiskey

1 tablespoon sweet vermouth

3 dashes Angostura bitters

Combine the cherries, water, sugar, and lemon juice in a medium saucepan set over medium high heat and cook, stirring occasionally, until the sugar has dissolved. Transfer the mixture to a blender or use an immersion blender to puree the mixture until smooth. Strain through a fine-mesh sieve, then whisk in the whiskey, vermouth, and bitters. Chill thoroughly, at least 4 hours or overnight, then freeze the mixture in an ice cream machine according to the manufacturer's instructions. Transfer the sorbet to a freezer-safe container, cover, and freeze until firm, about 4 hours or overnight. Keeps for four days.

CHERRY AND POPPY SEED YOGURT CAKE

| MAKES ONE 9 BY 5-INCH LOAF CAKE

STREUSEL

¼ cup (35g)
all purpose flour

2 tablespoons old-fashioned oats

2 tablespoons granulated sugar

2 teaspoons poppy seeds

Pinch salt

2 tablespoons unsalted butter, softened

CAKE

1½ cups all purpose flour

1½ teaspoons baking powder

2 tablespoons poppy seeds

½ teaspoon salt

¾ cup (150g) granulated sugar

½ cup (120ml) canola or grapeseed oil

3 large eggs, at room temperature

1 cup (225g) plain yogurt

¼ cup (60ml) freshly squeezed lime juice

2 limes, for zest

1½ cups (210g) pitted sweet or sour cherries

Quick loaf cakes like this one are some of my favorite things to bake, mostly because they are simple to put together, and they taste even better the next day. They are equally tasty as a teatime treat or simple dessert, or even served for breakfast. I love the crunchy texture of poppy seeds so much that I used them twice in this recipe both in the streusel topping and in the cake. Folding half of the cherries into the batter and sprinkling half on top ensures that every bite of cake, from top to bottom, will be filled with sweet, and jammy pockets of fruit.

Position a rack in the center of the oven and preheat to 350ºF (180ºC). Butter and flour a 9 by 5 by 3-inch loaf pan.

To make the streusel: In a small bowl, stir the flour, oats, sugar, poppy seeds, and salt together. Add in the butter and use your fingertips to mix until small crumbs form. Set aside while you prepare the cake batter.

To make the cake: Whisk the flour, baking powder, poppy seeds, and salt together in a small bowl. Add the sugar to a large bowl and grate about 1 tablespoon of lime zest directly into the sugar. Use your fingers to rub the zest into the sugar until evenly distributed. Add the oil, eggs, yogurt, and lime juice and whisk to combine. Add the flour mixture all at once, switch to a rubber spatula, and stir until just combined. Fold in half of the cherries.

Pour the batter into the prepared pan and scatter the remaining cherries over the top. Sprinkle the streusel in an even layer over the cherries. Bake the cake until puffed and golden and a cake tester inserted into the center comes out clean, 40 to 50 minutes. Let cool completely before slicing. This cake will keep in an airtight container for about three days at room temperature.

SEASONAL VARIATIONS: Substitute just about any berry or chopped stone fruit for the cherries here, and lemon juice and zest make a fine replacement for the lime.

summer

The summer market is wild with flavor and color. In the Northeast, we are lucky to have a wide variety of locally grown berries available, ranging from the usual blueberries, raspberries, and blackberries to the more rare black raspberries and mouth-puckering gooseberries and currants. Berries are wonderfully versatile because they taste great both cooked and raw—they're brilliant in desserts, and also make a fine snack for my subway rides home from the market during those hot summer months. Later in the season, the orchards begin to pop with stone fruits—sweet peaches and nectarines, juicy plums in every color, and rosy-cheeked apricots.

Despite the heat, I think summer is the best time of year to bake. The humidity in my apartment makes the task less pleasant, but I just can't help myself when there are so many picnics and barbecues and rooftop parties that call for dessert. Plus, when the mercury really starts to rise, there are plenty of other cooling treats to be made.

Freshly picked fruit can't be beat and one of my favorite summer activities is escaping the city to gather it. I am lucky to have friends with a little cabin by a creek in Accord, New York, which we visit often. We make time each day to stop by the U-pick farms for berries and stone fruits to complement whatever we grill over the wood fire for dinner. There are pick-your-own fruit farms all over the country, search for farms in your area (try www.pickyourown.org) and have a little adventure of your own.

APRICOTS

I NEVER TRULY APPRECIATED APRICOTS UNTIL I
STARTED BUYING THEM FROM THE FARMERS'
MARKET. THE ONES SOLD AT THE GROCERY STORE
ARE PICKED UNDER-RIPE, AND NEVER QUITE REACH
PEAK FLAVOR, BUT THE ONES AT THE FARMERS'
MARKET ARE TRULY LUSCIOUS. A PERFECT APRICOT
IS A THING OF BEAUTY WITH ITS ROSY CHEEKS,
VELVETY SKIN, AND RICH HONEYED SCENT. RIPE
APRICOTS ARE SLIGHTLY SOFT, AND YOU SHOULD
BE ABLE TO PULL THE TWO HALVES APART EASILY
TO REMOVE THE PITS, BUT HANDLE THEM GENTLY
AS THEY TEND TO BRUISE EASILY.

APRICOT AND BERRY GALETTE WITH SAFFRON SUGAR

| MAKES ONE 9-INCH GALETTE

This galette combines rosy-cheeked apricots with juicy dark berries for a stunning presentation: a study in complementary colors and flavors. The saffron sugar sounds supremely fancy, but it is quite simple to put together, and you only need a small amount of saffron to flavor the galette. The rye pie crust has a sweet, milky flavor and is a wonderful base for all types of fruit tarts and pies.

½ recipe (360g) Rye Pie Crust (see rye variation on All-Butter Pie Crust, page 228)

½ vanilla bean

3 tablespoons granulated sugar

Pinch saffron threads

2 teaspoons all purpose flour

Pinch salt

8 ounces (225g) apricots

½ cup (80g) blueberries

½ cup (80g) blackberries

¼ cup (60g) Small-Batch Apricot Jam (page 67)

1 large egg, lightly beaten for egg wash

1 tablespoon turbinado sugar

Line a large baking sheet with parchment paper. On a lightly floured surface, roll the dough into a roughly 12-inch circle, just under ¼-inch thick; it's okay if it isn't perfectly round. Transfer the dough to the prepared baking sheet. Store in the fridge while you prepare the filling.

Use the tip of a knife to cut the vanilla bean in half lengthwise and scrape out the seeds. Reserve the pod for another use. Add the granulated sugar to a mortar, add the vanilla seeds and saffron threads, and grind with a pestle until finely ground. The sugar will turn pale yellow and smell wonderful. Stir in the flour and salt.

Gently tear the apricots in half. Place the apricot halves into a large bowl and discard the pits. Add the berries and the saffron-vanilla sugar mixture to the bowl and toss with your hands to combine.

Remove the dough from the fridge and spread the jam on top, leaving a 2-inch border around the edges, then top with the fruit. Fold the edges of the pastry over the fruit and press gently to seal the folds. Chill the formed tart until the dough is firm, about 15 minutes.

Position a rack in the center of the oven and preheat to 400ºF (200ºC). When the tart is nice and cold remove it from the fridge and gently brush the dough with the egg wash; sprinkle with the turbinado sugar.

Bake until the fruit juices bubble and the pastry is deep golden brown, 30 to 40 minutes. Let cool slightly before serving. This tart is best served the day it's made.

SMALL-BATCH APRICOT JAM

| MAKES ABOUT 3 CUPS (680G)

If I had to choose only one preserve to put up each summer, it would be apricot jam. It is sweet and tart, and it's the perfect addition to fruit galettes and tarts. Because this recipe makes a relatively small amount of jam, I don't bother to process the jars to make them shelf stable. This recipe is endlessly adaptable, and you can use this general ratio for most berry and stone fruit jams, all summer long. Keep in mind that cooking times will vary depending on the variety of fruit.

1¼ pounds (560g) ripe apricots

1 cup plus 2 tablespoons (225g) granulated sugar

Juice of 1 lemon (about 3 tablespoons)

Place several teaspoons on a small plate in the freezer to chill. You will use these to test the jam for doneness.

Gently tear the apricots in half, place the fruit into a heavy-bottomed nonreactive pot, and discard the pits. Mash the apricots and sugar with a potato masher, fork, or your clean hands if you feel like it. Add the lemon juice and mix it in.

Bring the apricots to a boil over medium high heat. The jam will cook very quickly, so stir constantly with a rubber spatula to avoid scorching the bottom. Don't worry about skimming any foam that appears on the surface of the jam.

After about 10 minutes, the jam should be thick; it will spatter like hot lava, so watch your hands! Check for doneness by putting a small amount of jam on one of the cold spoons. Return the spoon to the plate in the freezer for one minute, then take it out and push the jam with your finger. If the surface wrinkles, it's done. If not, cook it for a few more minutes and test again using a different cold spoon. Once it's done, remove the pot from the heat and add any optional flavorings (see Variations, below).

Ladle the finished jam into clean jars, cool to room temperature, and refrigerate. The jam will keep, refrigerated, for one month.

VARIATIONS: Try adding the seeds of one vanilla bean or a few drops of rose water. Or soak 1/2 teaspoon of ground saffron in 2 tablespoons warm water. Add to the jam just after you pull it off of the heat.

ROASTED APRICOT AND BUTTERMILK SHERBET

| MAKES ABOUT 1 QUART (900G)

Roasting fruit is one of the best ways to coax all of its flavors to the surface, by caramelizing the fruit's natural sugars. It is also a great way to prepare fruit that is going to be turned into ice cream (or, in this case, sherbet) because it reduces the water content, which makes for a creamier final product. The combination of buttermilk and heavy cream makes this sherbet both tangy and rich.

1½ pounds (680g) apricots

¾ cup (150g) granulated sugar

2 tablespoons golden syrup or light corn syrup

1 cup (240ml) buttermilk

½ cup (120ml) heavy cream

¼ teaspoon salt

Position a rack in the center of the oven and preheat to 375ºF (190ºC).

Gently tear the apricots in half. Place the fruit on a baking sheet, and discard the pits. Sprinkle the sugar over the top and toss the apricots and sugar together. Bake the apricots, stirring once halfway through, until they are soft and their juices are beginning to caramelize, 15 to 20 minutes. Let the apricots cool to room temperature, then add them and their juices to a food processor or blender with the salt and golden syrup. Blend until smooth. Pass the mixture through a fine-mesh sieve to remove the skins, letting the juice and puree gather in a bowl.

Stir in the buttermilk and heavy cream and chill the mixture for at least 4 hours or overnight. When the mixture is thoroughly chilled, freeze in an ice cream machine according to the manufacturer's instructions. Transfer the sherbet to a freezer-safe container, cover, and freeze until firm, about 4 hours or overnight. Keeps for four days.

SEASONAL VARIATIONS: In the spring, substitute an equal amount of roasted strawberries. Roasted blueberries also make a delicious and beautiful substitute for the apricots.

MIXED BERRIES

BERRIES COME IN ENDLESS VARIETIES, WHICH SHOW UP AT THE MARKET IN TURN ALL SUMMER LONG, EACH MORE BEAUTIFUL AND TASTY THAN THE LAST. LOOK FOR FIRM, PLUMP BERRIES WITHOUT ANY SURFACE WRINKLES, WHICH INDICATE THE FRUIT IS LESS THAN FRESH. I GREW UP PICKING THE BLACKBERRIES THAT GROW WILD ALL OVER MY HOMETOWN OF SEATTLE EVERY JULY AND AUGUST, BUT MY MOST MEMORABLE BERRY PICKING EXPERIENCE WAS AT RADKE'S BLUEBERRIES NEAR CORVALLIS, OREGON, WHERE THE BERRIES THE SIZE OF GRAPES GROW IN STUNNING CLUSTERS AND ARE SWEET AS CAN BE. IF YOU ARE PICKING YOUR OWN BERRIES, MAKE SURE TO ONLY PICK FRUIT THAT IS RIPE AND SWEET, AS BERRIES WILL NOT RIPEN FURTHER ONCE PICKED.

BLUEBERRY SKILLET COBBLER WITH WHOLE WHEAT BISCUITS

| MAKES ONE 10-INCH COBBLER

BLUEBERRIES

6 cups (960g) blueberries

⅓ cup (67g) granulated sugar

1 tablespoon cornstarch

Juice from ½ lemon (about 4 teaspoons)

1 teaspoon lemon zest

½ teaspoon orange zest

¼ teaspoon freshly grated nutmeg

WHOLE WHEAT BISCUITS

1 cup (130g) whole wheat flour

½ cup (63g) all purpose flour

¼ cup (50g) granulated sugar

2 teaspoons baking powder

¼ teaspoon baking soda

¼ teaspoon salt

¼ cup (60g) unsalted butter, melted and cooled

½ cup (120ml) buttermilk

½ cup (120ml) heavy cream

½ teaspoon vanilla extract (page 235)

2 teaspoons turbinado sugar

Vanilla ice cream, to serve

Cobbler is one of those homey desserts that certainly tastes better than it looks. This version is a classic, made from juicy blueberries delicately spiced and topped with fluffy whole wheat buttermilk biscuits.

To make the blueberries: Position a rack in the center of the oven and preheat to 375ºF (190ºC). Butter a 10-inch cast-iron skillet. Combine the blueberries, sugar, cornstarch, lemon juice and zest, orange zest, and nutmeg in a large bowl. Stir gently to combine evenly. Pour the blueberry mixture into the skillet.

To make the biscuits: In a clean bowl, whisk together the flours, sugar, baking powder, baking soda, and salt. In a measuring cup, combine the buttermilk, cream, and vanilla. Add the melted butter and stir gently.

Make a well in the center of the dry ingredients and pour in the buttermilk mixture. Use a rubber spatula to stir the ingredients together until just combined. The biscuit dough will be soft and sticky.

Use two spoons or a spring-loaded ice cream scoop to dollop the biscuit dough on top of the blueberries in 8 even pieces. The dough will rise and expand in the oven, so leave a bit of room in between the pieces. Brush the tops of the biscuits with the dregs of liquid left in the measuring cup, then sprinkle with the turbinado sugar.

Move the pan to a large baking sheet to catch any drips and slide the pan into the oven. Bake for 30 to 35 minutes, or until the biscuits are golden and cooked through and the fruit is bubbling. Serve warm with vanilla ice cream or whipped cream. This cobbler is best the day it's made, but it makes a great breakfast the next day, too.

SEASONAL VARIATIONS: Cobbler is one of the most versatile fruit desserts. Try apples and pears with warm spices in the fall, strawberries or rhubarb in the spring, and cranberries in the winter.

CRÈME FRAÎCHE AND BLUEBERRY ICE CREAM

| MAKES ABOUT ONE QUART (900G)

In this ice cream, the subtle tang of crème fraîche paired with sweet roasted blueberry sauce is not only gorgeous, but also creates a lovely play of sweet and tart flavors. Crème fraîche is French-style sour cream that can easily be made at home if you can't find it in your local grocery.

4 egg yolks

1 cup (240ml) whole milk

1 cup (240ml) heavy cream

1¼ cups (250g) granulated sugar; divided

Pinch salt

1 cup (225g) Crème Fraîche (page 229)

1 cup (160g) blueberries

2 tablespoons golden syrup or light corn syrup

1 tablespoon lemon juice

To make the ice cream: Whisk the egg yolks together in a glass or stainless steel bowl; set aside. Combine the milk, cream, 1 cup of the sugar, and salt in a saucepan. Cook over medium heat, stirring occasionally, until the mixture begins to bubble around the edges, about 5 minutes.

Ladle about 1 cup of the cream mixture into the egg yolks and whisk vigorously. Pour the egg and cream mixture back into the pan and whisk well to combine. Cook the mixture on medium low heat, stirring constantly with a rubber spatula, being careful not to let the mixture boil. Cook until the mixture thickens enough to coat the back of a spoon, about 7 minutes. Turn off the heat and whisk in the crème fraîche until smooth. Strain the mixture through a fine-mesh sieve and cool completely in the refrigerator, at least 4 hours or overnight.

To make the blueberry sauce: Combine the berries, the remaining ¼ cup of sugar, golden syrup, and lemon juice in a saucepan and mash with a potato masher. Cook over medium high heat, stirring occasionally, until the blueberry juices reduce to a syrupy consistency, 5 to 7 minutes. You should have about ¾ cup of blueberry sauce. Transfer the blueberry sauce to a bowl, cover, and chill thoroughly.

Freeze the ice cream mixture in an ice cream machine according to the manufacturer's instructions. While the ice cream is churning, remove the blueberry sauce from the fridge and stir it well. Working quickly, spoon ⅓ of the ice cream into a freezer-safe container (I like to use a loaf pan), drizzle half of the blueberries over the top, and repeat the process, finishing with a layer of ice cream. Cover and freeze until firm, about 4 hours or overnight. Keeps for four days.

CURRANT AND GOOSEBERRY BUCKLE

| MAKES ONE 9-INCH CAKE

CRISP TOPPING

5 tablespoons (70g) cold unsalted butter

½ cup plus 2 tablespoons (80g) all purpose flour

⅓ cup (40g) sliced almonds

¼ cup (50g) granulated sugar

¼ teaspoon salt

CAKE

1½ cups (190g) all purpose flour

1½ teaspoons baking soda

½ teaspoon baking powder

¾ teaspoon salt

12 tablespoons (170g) unsalted butter, softened

¾ cup (150g) sugar

½ teaspoon lemon zest

3 large eggs, at room temperature

1 cup (225g) full-fat yogurt or sour cream, at room temperature

½ teaspoon vanilla extract (page 235)

¼ teaspoon almond extract

2½ cups (300g) mixed red or green gooseberries and red or white currants

Buckles, with all of their lumps and bumps, may not win any beauty contests, but they truly are a best-of-both-worlds kind of dessert. Half fruit cake and half fruit crisp, buckles are comprised of dense cake batter packed with so much fruit that it "buckles" from the weight, and then is finished with buttery, crisp topping. If currants and gooseberries are not available where you live, you can use a combination of any other tart berries.

Position a rack in the center of the oven and preheat to 350ºF (180ºC). Butter a 9-inch cake pan or springform pan with high sides, at least 2- inches tall, and line it with parchment paper. Butter the paper, then dust the pan and paper with flour.

To make the topping: Stir the flour, almonds, sugar, and salt together in a medium bowl. Add the butter and mix with your fingers until it is well combined and crumbs form. Set aside while you prepare the cake.

To make the cake: Whisk the flour, baking soda, baking powder, and salt together in a small bowl.

In the bowl of a stand mixer fitted with the paddle attachment, or in a large bowl with a handheld electric mixer, cream the butter and sugar together with the lemon zest until light and fluffy, about 5 minutes. Add the eggs, one at a time, beating for 30 seconds after each addition. Add the yogurt, followed by the extracts and lemon zest. Add the flour mixture all at once and stir until just combined. The batter will be very thick.

CONTINUED

Pour half of the cake batter into the prepared pan. Scatter half of the fruit on top. Spoon the remaining cake batter over the top, followed by the rest of the fruit. Finally, sprinkle the crisp topping evenly over the surface. Slide the cake into the oven and bake for 45 to 55 minutes, or until the cake is golden brown and a toothpick inserted into the center comes out clean. Extra buckle will keep in an airtight container at room temperature for up to two days.

SEASONAL VARIATIONS: In the fall and winter, substitute an equal amount of cranberries for the gooseberries and currants, and in the spring try tart or sweet cherries. Blueberries and blackberries also work well in this cake-meets-crisp.

BLACKBERRY AND SAGE CREAM PUFFS

| MAKES 12 BIG PUFFS

CREAM PUFFS

1 cup (240ml) water

6 tablespoons (85g) unsalted butter

1 tablespoon granulated sugar

¼ teaspoon salt

½ cup (63g) all purpose flour

½ cup (65g) rye flour

5 large eggs

1 tablespoon pearl sugar or turbinado sugar

BLACKBERRIES

3 cups (480g) blackberries

¼ cup (60g) granulated sugar

2 tablespoons lemon juice

4 large sage leaves

TOPPING

1 cup (240ml) heavy cream

½ cup (115g) mascarpone

2 teaspoons granulated sugar

1 teaspoon vanilla extract (page 235)

Cream puffs are a super classic and impressive-looking French dessert that actually come together fairly quickly. I love the flavor of rye flour with berries, so I have added some to the dough here, but you can omit it and just double the amount of all purpose flour if you prefer. Fill each puff with a generous spoonful of sage-scented blackberries and mascarpone whipped cream, and you've got a spectacular dessert for your next dinner party.

Position a rack in the center of the oven and preheat to 425ºF (220ºC). Line a baking sheet with parchment paper or a silicone mat.

To make the cream puffs: Combine the water, butter, sugar, and salt in a 2-quart saucepan. Heat over medium heat until the butter has melted completely and the mixture comes to a full rolling boil.

Remove the pan from the heat and add all of the flour at once. Stir vigorously with a wooden spoon until the mixture transforms to a smooth ball of dough that pulls away from the sides of the pan. Let the mixture cool for a few minutes. Add 4 of the eggs, one at a time, stirring to incorporate each egg completely before adding the next one.

Spoon the mixture into a pastry bag fitted with a large round tip (or a ziptop bag with the corner cut off) and pipe 12 even mounds at least 2 inches apart, onto the baking sheet. Wet your finger with a bit of water and use your fingertip to smooth any peaks or rough edges.

In a small bowl, beat the remaining egg and brush each mound with the egg. Sprinkle a few grains of pearl sugar on the top of each mound and bake for 25 to 30 minutes, or until golden brown all over and puffed. Cool completely before filling.

CONTINUED

BLACKBERRY AND SAGE CREAM PUFFS, CONTINUED

To make the blackberries: Combine 2 cups of the blackberries with ¼ cup of the sugar and the lemon juice in a saucepan. Mash the mixture thoroughly with a potato masher or fork. Add the sage leaves and bring the mixture to a boil over medium high heat. Cook the blackberries, stirring occasionally, until thickened and jammy, 7 to 10 minutes. Let the blackberries cool to room temperature, then remove the sage leaves and fold in the remaining 1 cup of blackberries. Store in the refrigerator until you are ready to serve.

To make the topping: In a large bowl with an electric mixer or in the bowl of a stand mixer, whip the cream, remaining 2 teaspoons of sugar, and vanilla to soft peaks. Whip in the mascarpone until medium peaks form. Store in the refrigerator until you are ready to serve.

To assemble: Slice each cream puff in half horizontally. Stir the blackberry mixture to loosen it, if necessary. Spoon about 3 tablespoons of the blackberry mixture onto the bottom half of the cream puff, followed by a spoonful of cream. Replace the top of the puff and repeat with the remaining puffs. Serve immediately.

BLACK FRUIT TART

| MAKES ONE 10-INCH TART

Slightly bitter buckwheat complements the sweet flavors of the mascarpone-enriched pastry cream and late summer fruit in this visually stunning tart. You could top this tart with any fruit you like, but I particularly like the combination of the deep, dark fruit and berries that are available at the end of the summer: blackberries, blueberries, Mission figs, Concord grapes, sliced black plums, and black raspberries (if you are lucky enough to find them) are all wonderful. If you use Concord grapes, make sure to tell your guests to watch for the seeds. Both the tart shell and the filling can be made in advance so you can assemble the tart just before serving, ensuring that the crust stays crisp.

Buckwheat Tart Shell (page 233), fully baked in a 10-inch (25cm) round pan and cooled

2 cups (450g) Pastry Cream, chilled (page 230)

1 cup (225g) mascarpone

½ cup (120ml) heavy cream

4 cups (450g) assorted dark-hued fruit and berries, such as blackberries, blueberries, Concord grapes, black plums, Mission figs, and black raspberries

To make the mascarpone cream: Whip the pastry cream until smooth, then add the mascarpone and beat until well combined. In a separate bowl, whip the heavy cream to stiff peaks, then fold it into the pastry cream.

To assemble: Fill the cooled tart shell with mascarpone cream and refrigerate for at least one hour. Top the cream with the fruit just before serving. This tart is best served the day it's made, as the shell will soften over time.

MELONS

MOST FOLKS HAVE ONLY BEEN EXPOSED TO A FEW VARIETIES OF MELON—PERHAPS CANTALOUPE, HONEYDEW, AND WATERMELON—BUT MELONS ACTUALLY GROW IN MANY VARIETIES. I KNOW THIS BECAUSE MY DAD IS A MELON NUT. EVERY SUMMER HE VISITS JUST ABOUT EVERY PRODUCE MARKET IN TOWN TO GET THE BEST SELECTION OF SANTA CLAUS MELONS, CHARENTAIS MELONS WITH CORAL-COLORED INTERIORS, CRENSHAWS, ORANGE HONEYDEW, AND EXCEPTIONALLY SWEET YELLOW AND ORANGE WATERMELON VARIETIES. WHILE THEY ARE ALL DELICIOUS CHILLED AND SLICED, TURNING THEM INTO SOMETHING A LITTLE MORE SPECIAL IS A LOVELY WAY TO CELEBRATE THEIR FRESH FLAVOR. CHOOSE MELONS THAT ARE HEAVY FOR THEIR SIZE, WHICH INDICATES THAT THEY ARE VERY JUICY.

CANTALOUPE AND MINT YOGURT POPS

| MAKES 6 TO 12 POPS, DEPENDING ON THE SIZE OF THE MOLDS

Chilled melon sprinkled with rose or orange-flower water is a classic and very cooling Middle Eastern dessert, wonderful on a hot day. These ice pops take that flavor combination and add tart Greek yogurt and brightly flavored mint for an extra refreshing frozen treat, perfect for the dog days of summer. This mixture can also be thoroughly chilled, then churned in an ice cream machine and served immediately as soft-serve frozen yogurt.

12 ounces (340g) seeded and chopped cantaloupe

1 cup (225g) 2 percent or full-fat Greek yogurt

⅓ cup (80ml) mild honey, or more to taste

1 tablespoon mint leaves, packed

1 teaspoon orange-flower water

Combine all the ingredients in a blender or food processor and blend until smooth. Taste the mixture and adjust the level of sweetness if necessary by adding more honey, one teaspoon at time. Pour into frozen pop molds and freeze the pops until completely firm, at least 6 hours or overnight.

WATERMELON GRANITA WITH CHILE AND LIME

| MAKES ABOUT 4 CUPS

In the summer, street vendors all over New York serve watermelon cubes and fresh mangoes sliced into flower shapes, always accompanied by a little condiment bar with salt, chile powder, cayenne, and a bit of bottled citrus juice. This icy granita combines all of those flavors for a sweet, salty, and cooling treat. It is also delicious with a shot of tequila or smoky mezcal poured over the top. An equal amount of sliced mango can be substituted for the watermelon.

1 pound (450g) chopped seedless watermelon

¼ cup (60ml) freshly squeezed lime juice

⅓ cup (67g) granulated sugar

¼ teaspoon salt, plus more to serve

¼ teaspoon chile powder

⅛ teaspoon cayenne pepper, or more to taste

Lime wedges, to serve

Combine the watermelon, lime juice, sugar, salt, chile powder, and cayenne in a blender or food processor and blend on high until smooth. Pour the mixture into a 9 by 13-inch glass or metal dish and cover with plastic wrap. Slide the dish into the freezer and chill for one hour. Remove the dish from the freezer and scrape the surface with a fork to break up the crystals, cover, and place back in the freezer. Scrape the granita every hour or so until it is completely frozen and crystals have formed throughout. Serve in clear glasses topped with a pinch of salt and a squeeze of lime. The granita will keep for about five days, covered, in the freezer.

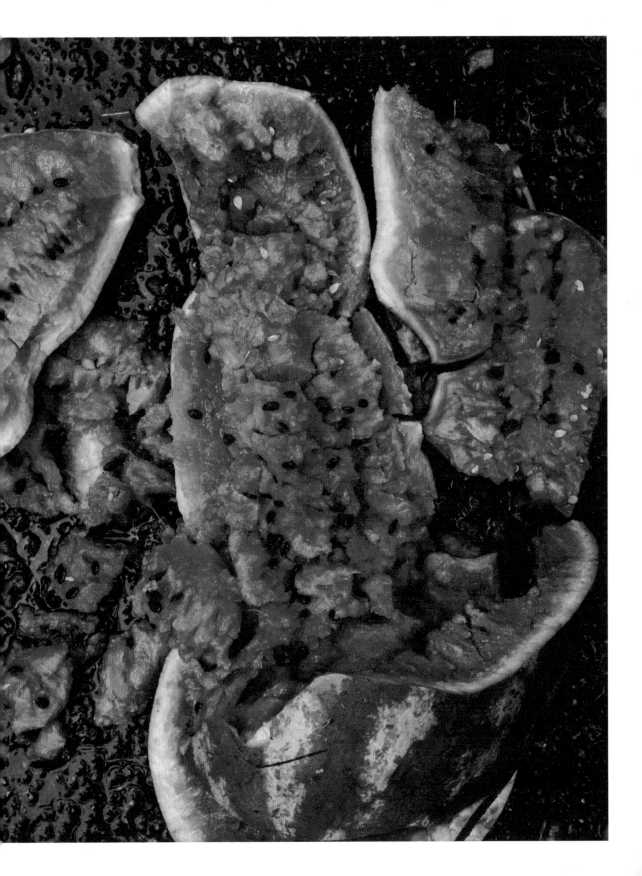

STONE FRUITS

LATE SUMMER BRINGS AN IMPRESSIVE ARRAY OF STONE FRUIT TO THE MARKET: PEACHES, NECTARINES, PLUMS, AND HYBRIDS IN EVERY SHADE. PERFECTLY RIPE STONE FRUIT IS SOFT AND YIELDING, JUICY AND FRAGRANT. WHITE AND YELLOW PEACHES, AND NECTARINE VARIETIES ALL MAKE LUSCIOUS DESSERTS.

MY FAVORITE PLUMS FOR BAKING ARE ITALIAN PLUMS, THEY ARE OBLONG WITH DEEP PURPLE SKIN AND YELLOW FLESH WHICH HOLDS UP VERY WELL TO COOKING. THERE IS A PLUM TREE IN MY PARENTS' BACKYARD THAT WAS ONCE QUITE PROLIFIC, BUT HAS SINCE BEEN SHADED BY AN ENORMOUS BIRCH TREE. NO MATTER THOUGH, AS FRIENDS ALWAYS SEEM TO HAVE PLUM TREES THAT PRODUCE ENOUGH FRUIT THAT WE ARE GIFTED WITH PAPER GROCERY BAGS FULL EVERY SUMMER.

NECTARINE AND BLACKBERRY PIE BARS

| MAKES ABOUT 24 BARS

Crisp Topping, whole wheat variation (page 230)

CRUST

¾ cup (170g) unsalted butter

1 cup (125g) all purpose flour

1 cup (130g) whole wheat flour

⅓ cup (60g) firmly packed light brown sugar

¾ teaspoon salt

FILLING

1¼ pounds (560g) nectarines (about 4 medium)

½ vanilla bean, or 1 teaspoon vanilla extract (page 235)

¼ cup (50g) sugar (less if the fruit is particularly sweet)

½ teaspoon lemon zest

½ teaspoon ground cinnamon

¼ teaspoon freshly grated nutmeg

2 tablespoons all purpose flour

Pinch salt

1¼ cups (200g) blackberries

These crowd-pleasing pie bars are just the thing to take to a summer barbecue: you can make them ahead of time, they travel well, and the recipe is big enough to feed a backyard full of friends. I've made these bars with just about every stone fruit that exists, but this version, with sweet, thin-skinned nectarines and tart blackberries, is a favorite. If you have one, use a metal quarter sheet pan to bake these bars rather than a glass baking dish—the low sides allow for even browning on the crisp topping and no soggy edges.

Position a rack in the center of the oven and preheat to 350ºF (180ºC). Line a 9 by 13-inch baking pan or a quarter sheet pan with aluminum foil. Lightly grease the foil.

To make the crust: Melt the butter in a light-colored saucepan over medium heat, stirring occasionally, until the foam subsides, the milk solids turn light brown, and the butter has a warm and nutty fragrance, about 5 minutes. Remove the butter to a heat-safe container and let it cool to room temperature.

In a large bowl, combine the flours, sugar, and salt. Pour in the cooled butter and stir gently until a ball forms. Pat the dough evenly into the prepared pan. Bake the crust until light golden brown, about 20 minutes. Set aside to cool while you prepare the filling.

To make the filling: Pit and coarsely chop the nectarines. Use the tip of a knife to slice the vanilla bean lengthwise and scrape out the seeds; reserve the pod for another use. Add the sugar, vanilla seeds, and lemon zest to a large bowl and use your fingers to rub the vanilla seeds and zest into the sugar. Stir in the spices, flour, and salt. Add the nectarines and blackberries to the sugar mixture and toss gently to combine. Pour over the partially cooled crust. Sprinkle the crisp topping evenly over the top.

Bake the bars until the topping is golden brown and the fruit begins to release its juices, 30 to 40 minutes. Cool completely before slicing.

WINE-SOAKED PEACHES WITH LEMON VERBENA

| SERVES 6-8

There's nothing better than eating a perfectly ripe peach, hunched over the kitchen sink, with the juices dripping down your arms. But let's face it, that perfect peach moment is hard to achieve, even during the height of summer. This recipe makes perfect peaches truly heavenly and the ones that are less so, close to divine. This dessert is light and refreshing and gets better after a long rest in the refrigerator, making it perfect for a summer dinner party. Do yourself a favor and seek out freestone peaches for this recipe, as they are much easier to pit and slice than clingstone varieties.

1 vanilla bean

½ cup (100g) granulated sugar

8 large lemon verbena leaves

6 medium yellow or white peaches, firm but ripe, about 1 pound (450g)

1 (750ml) bottle crisp, dry white wine, like Sauvignon Blanc

Lightly sweetened whipped cream, to serve

Use the tip of a knife to slice the vanilla bean in half lengthwise and scrape out the seeds. In a large bowl, rub the vanilla seeds into the sugar with your fingers until well combined and fragrant, add the vanilla bean pod as well. Tear the lemon verbena leaves in half and crush them with your fingers to release their fragrance and oils. Add them to the sugar then whisk in the wine.

Wash and gently scrub the peaches to remove some of their fuzz. Slice the peaches in half to remove the pits, then slice each half into ½-inch wedges, adding the wedges to the wine mixture as you go. The peaches should be completely submerged in the wine mixture. If they aren't, either move them to a smaller container or top off the mixture with a bit more wine. Cover and refrigerate at least overnight and up to two days. Stir the peaches occasionally to help the sugar dissolve. The peaches will become more flavorful as they sit. Serve about one peach per person in clear glasses topped with a bit of the chilled wine syrup and a dollop of cream, if you like.

Use any leftover peach-scented wine syrup to make a refreshing spritzer: fill a glass with ice, then fill it three-quarters full of wine, and top the whole thing off with a splash of sparkling water and a lemon twist. Cheers!

SPELT SHORTCAKES WITH ROASTED STONE FRUIT

| MAKES 8 SHORTCAKES

SHORTCAKES

1 cup (130g) spelt flour

1 cup (125g)
all purpose flour

2 tablespoons
granulated sugar

1 tablespoon baking
powder

¼ teaspoon baking soda

¼ teaspoon salt

6 tablespoons (85g) cold
unsalted butter, cubed

¾ cup (180ml) heavy
cream, cold

¼ cup (60ml) buttermilk,
cold

1 tablespoon
turbinado sugar

ROASTED FRUIT

2 pounds (900g)
assorted stone fruit
(peaches, plums, cherries,
nectarines, apricots)

⅓ cup (80ml) mild honey

¼ teaspoon ground
cardamom

1 bay leaf

Pinch of black pepper

TO SERVE

1½ cups (360ml) heavy
cream

2 teaspoons granulated
sugar

Shortcakes are one of the most underrated desserts. I'm sure we've all had a subpar strawberry shortcake with those weird, spongy store-bought cakes, but they can be so much more. For this summer version, I made wholesome spelt biscuits and roasted a pile of stone fruit, and topped the fruit with a dollop of lightly sweetened cream.

Position a rack in the center of the oven and preheat to 375ºF (190ºC). Line a baking sheet with parchment paper.

To make the shortcakes: In a large bowl, whisk the flours, sugar, baking powder, baking soda, and salt together until well combined. Cut the cold butter into the dry ingredients using a pastry blender or your fingers until it is the size of peas. Make a well in the center of the mixture then add in the heavy cream and buttermilk. Stir gently until just combined. It's okay if there are a few dry spots—it is best not to overmix this type of dough. If it seems very dry or at all sandy, add more cream or buttermilk, one tablespoon at a time.

Turn the dough out onto a lightly floured surface and pat it into a square about 1 inch thick. Fold the dough in half over itself and again pat into a square about 1 inch thick. Repeat this process one more time, then cut the dough into eight even squares and transfer the squares to the prepared baking sheet. Put the whole baking sheet into the freezer for 10 minutes.

Just before baking, brush the tops of the shortcakes with the dregs of liquid left in the measuring cup and sprinkle with the turbinado sugar. Bake until the tops are browned and the shortcakes are cooked through, 20 to 25 minutes.

CONTINUED

SPELT SHORTCAKES WITH ROASTED STONE FRUIT, CONTINUED

To roast the fruit: Pit cherries and quarter plums and apricots, cut peaches or nectarines into roughly ½-inch wedges. Pile all the fruit onto a baking sheet and drizzle the honey over the top; add the cardamom, bay leaf, and black pepper. Stir gently to combine. Bake the fruit until it has begun to release its juices and caramelize slightly, 12 to 15 minutes, stirring halfway through. Remove the bay leaf and let the fruit cool slightly before assembling.

To assemble: Whip the cream and sugar to soft peaks. Carefully slice each shortcake in half horizontally. They are delicate and might crack, but don't worry it they do—the fruit and cream will hold the whole luscious mess together. Top the bottom half of each shortcake with a generous spoonful of fruit and juices and a dollop of whipped cream, then replace the tops. Serve immediately. These shortcakes are best on the day they are baked. Extra fruit will keep in the refrigerator for three days.

SEASONAL VARIATIONS: Try roasted rhubarb with ginger and vanilla in the spring or roasted apples and pears with a bit of cinnamon and allspice in the fall and winter. Lightly sweetened fresh berries of just about any variety would also be welcome here.

PLUM PIE WITH HAZELNUT CRUMB

| MAKES ONE 9-INCH PIE

½ recipe (360g) Rye Pie Crust (see rye variation on All-Butter Pie Crust, page 228)

HAZELNUT CRUMB

¼ cup (55g) unsalted butter

½ cup (70g) chopped hazelnuts

¼ cup (32g) rye flour

2 tablespoons all purpose flour

3 tablespoons light brown sugar, firmly packed

¼ teaspoon salt

½ teaspoon ground cinnamon

FILLING

2 pounds (900g) Italian plums, ripe but firm

½ cup (100g) granulated sugar

¼ cup (32g) all purpose flour

½ teaspoon ground cinnamon

1 vanilla bean, or 2 teaspoons vanilla extract (page 235)

Juice of ½ lemon (about 4 teaspoons)

TO SERVE

Vanilla ice cream or lightly sweetened whipped cream

Plum pies aren't particularly common, but I love how tart plum skins and sweet flesh soften as they cook into this lightly spiced pie. The crumb topping is rich and toasty thanks to the combination of browned butter and a generous amount of hazelnuts. Use ripe but firm Italian plums for this pie, as they contain less water than other plum varieties and hold up very well to cooking.

Position a rack in the lower third of the oven and preheat to 375ºF (190ºC).

To make the hazelnut crumb: Melt the butter in a saucepan over medium heat. Stir occasionally until the milk solids turn light brown and the butter has a warm and nutty fragrance, about 5 minutes. Remove the butter to a heat-safe container and let it cool to room temperature.

In a large bowl, stir the chopped hazelnuts, flours, brown sugar, salt, and cinnamon together. Stir in the cooled butter until the ingredients are evenly combined and crumbs form.

Roll the pie crust out to a 12-inch circle ⅛ to ¼ inch thick. Trim any rough edges, then move it to a 9-inch pie pan, fold the edges under, and crimp in a decorative pattern. Refrigerate the crust while you make the filling.

To make the filling: Use the tip of a knife to slice the vanilla bean lengthwise and scrape out the seeds; reserve the pod for another use. Add the vanilla seeds and sugar to a large bowl. Use your fingers to rub the vanilla seeds into the sugar. Stir in the flour and cinnamon. Pit and chop the plums into roughly ½-inch pieces. Add the plums and lemon juice to the bowl. Stir gently to combine. Pour the filling into the chilled crust then scatter the crumbs over the top. Transfer the pie to a baking sheet to catch any drips, and bake for 45 to 55 minutes, or until the crumbs are deep golden brown and the filling is bubbly. Cool slightly before serving with ice cream or whipped cream.

RASPBERRIES

MY PARENTS HAVE A LITTLE PLOT OF RASPBERRY
BUSHES IN THEIR BACKYARD THAT I LOVE TO WATCH
GROW AND RIPEN EVERY SUMMER. MY MOM EVEN
SENDS ME PHOTOS WHEN I CAN'T MAKE IT TO
SEATTLE TO SEE THEM IN PERSON. THE BERRIES
THEY GROW ARE TINY AND DEEP MAGENTA, WITH
A PUNCHY, SWEET FLAVOR THAT IS UNMATCHED
BY STORE-BOUGHT VARIETIES. I DIDN'T REALIZE
WHAT A SPECIAL TREAT IT WAS TO EAT THEM EVERY
JULY, WARM FROM THE SUN, UNTIL I MOVED AWAY
FROM HOME. FRESHLY PICKED RASPBERRIES ARE
FRAGILE AND PRECIOUS, SO THEY ARE BEST STORED
IN THE REFRIGERATOR, UNWASHED, IN A SINGLE
LAYER. IF YOU ARE LUCKY ENOUGH TO PICK YOUR
OWN RASPBERRIES, MAKE SURE TO EAT SOME
STRAIGHT AWAY.

COCONUT CREAM FOOL WITH RASPBERRIES

| SERVES 6-8

Fool is a traditional British dessert made from whipped cream folded with sweetened berries and it's possibly the easiest dessert ever, with the exception of a raw piece of fruit eaten out of hand. This riff on a classic fool uses whipped coconut cream in place of the dairy cream for a vegan treat that is equal parts light and luxurious. This dessert is best prepared and served immediately. Don't forget to plan ahead: the coconut milk must be refrigerated at least overnight so the cream can be easily scraped from the top and whipped; put the bowl of your stand mixer in the freezer as well. For a dairy version, substitute 2 cups (480ml) of heavy cream for the coconut milk.

3 cups (450g) raspberries

3 tablespoons granulated sugar, plus more to taste

1 teaspoon rose water

2 (14-ounce/414ml) cans cold full-fat coconut milk, chilled overnight

½ teaspoon almond extract

1 teaspoon vanilla extract (page 235)

Toasted coconut flakes, to serve (optional)

Gently mash two cups of the berries with 1 tablespoon of the sugar and the rose water in a medium bowl. Taste and adjust the sweetness by adding a bit more sugar as necessary. Chill while you whip the coconut cream.

Turn the cold cans of coconut milk upside down, open the cans, and pour the coconut liquid into a storage container (save it for smoothies!). There should be a thick layer of coconut cream on the bottom of each can. Scoop the chilled cream from the cans into the chilled bowl of a stand mixer fitted with the whisk attachment or a large bowl and whip on medium high until the cream thickens into medium stiff peaks. Whip in the remaining 2 tablespoons of sugar, and the vanilla and almond extracts. Fold the berry mixture into the whipped coconut cream until just combined.

To serve: Layer the fool with the remaining cup of fresh berries in clear glass dishes. Top with coconut flakes, if desired, and serve immediately.

SEASONAL VARIATIONS: You can use just about any fresh berries to make a fool: blackberries with a bit of lime zest or currants are favorites. Spiced Rhubarb Compote (page 240) is also nice in the spring before berry season starts.

CHOCOLATE CELEBRATION CAKE WITH FRESH RASPBERRY BUTTERCREAM

| MAKES ONE 8-INCH LAYER CAKE

CHOCOLATE CAKE

2 cups (400g) granulated sugar

1¾ cups (225g) all purpose flour

¾ cup (75g) cocoa powder

1½ teaspoons baking powder

1½ teaspoons baking soda

1¼ teaspoon salt

1 cup (240ml) buttermilk, at room temperature

½ cup (120ml) grapeseed oil

⅓ cup (75g) full-fat plain yogurt, at room temperature

2 large eggs, at room temperature

2 teaspoons vanilla extract (page 235)

¾ cup (180ml) strong, hot coffee

INGREDIENTS CONTINUED

This is a legendary chocolate cake. It's the cake I make for just about every birthday and cake-serving occasion, of which there are many. It is fudgy and moist, and in this iteration it is perfectly offset with a pile of gorgeous and tangy red-raspberry buttercream. This buttercream is a Swiss-style buttercream, which may be new for some folks, but buttercreams made in this style are light, fluffy, and very smooth. This chocolate cake keeps very well in the freezer, wrapped in two layers of plastic wrap, for up to two weeks, so feel free to make it ahead of time. Just be sure to let the cake come to room temperature before decorating and serving.

Position a rack in the center of the oven and preheat to 350ºF (180ºC). Butter three 8-inch cake pans and line them with parchment paper. Butter the paper, too, then dust the pans with flour. This cake is sticky, so don't be tempted to skip the parchment paper.

To make the cake: Sift the sugar, flour, cocoa, baking soda, baking powder, and salt into a large bowl or the bowl of a stand mixer fitted with the paddle attachment, and stir to combine.

In a bowl or pitcher, whisk the milk, oil, yogurt, eggs, and vanilla together. With the mixer on low, pour the liquid mixture into the dry mixture and stir until the dry ingredients are well moistened. Stop the mixer, scrape down to the bottom of the bowl to make sure all of the dry ingredients are incorporated, then turn the mixer up to medium high and mix for 2 minutes.

Turn the mixer back down to low and slowly pour in the coffee. Stop the mixer and scrape down the bottom and sides of the bowl and finish mixing by hand. The batter will be quite thin.

CONTINUED

CHOCOLATE CELEBRATION CAKE WITH FRESH RASPBERRY BUTTERCREAM, CONTINUED

RASPBERRY BUTTERCREAM

8 ounces (225g) raspberries

5 large egg whites

1¼ cups (250g) granulated sugar

Pinch salt

2 cups (450g) unsalted butter, soft but cool, cut into tablespoon-size pieces

TO FINISH

8 ounces (225g) raspberries

Divide the mixture among the prepared pans and bake for 20 to 25 minutes, or until a cake tester comes out clean. Let the cakes cool in their pans set on a rack for 15 minutes, then invert them onto the rack to cool completely.

To make the buttercream: Use an immersion blender or potato masher to puree the raspberries, then pass the puree through a fine mesh sieve. Discard the seeds and any remaining solids.

In the bowl of a stand mixer or a large heat-safe bowl, whisk the egg whites and sugar together. Place the bowl over a pan of simmering water, ensuring that the bottom of the bowl does not touch the water, but rests just above it. Cook the egg whites and sugar, whisking often, until the sugar dissolves and the egg whites are syrupy and very hot to the touch.

Remove the egg whites from the double boiler and, with the whisk attachment, whip on high speed until stiff glossy peaks form and the mixture has cooled to room temperature, 7 to 10 minutes. Add the salt. Switch to the paddle attachment and turn the mixer down to medium low. Slowly add the butter to the meringue, tablespoon by tablespoon. During this step, it is likely that the frosting will "break," and you will think you have messed up. Good news: you didn't. Mine breaks sometimes, too. All you have to do is turn up the speed on the mixer for a few seconds and the buttercream will come back together.

After all of the butter has been incorporated and the buttercream is smooth and fluffy, very slowly stream in the raspberry puree and mix until well combined.

To assemble: Peel the parchment paper from the cake layers and trim them so the tops are flat. Place one layer on a serving platter or pedestal and spread about 1 cup of the buttercream onto the cake in an even layer, arrange half of the remaining raspberries evenly over the top. Place the second layer on top and repeat, but save a few fresh berries for the top of the cake. Finish by placing the last layer on top, trimmed side down, so the top of the cake will be nice and flat and crumb free. Cover the top and sides of the cake with a thin layer of frosting to seal in all of the crumbs. Refrigerate for about 30 minutes. Pull the cake out of the fridge and add a second, heavier coat of frosting to the top and sides of the cake. Top with the reserved fresh raspberries. Serve the cake at room temperature. Store any extra frosting in an airtight container in the freezer where it will keep for a few weeks. The cake will keep in the refrigerator for up to four days.

RASPBERRY SORBET WITH PINK PEPPERCORNS

| MAKES ABOUT 1 QUART (900G)

The summer after my junior year of college, my Aunt Guiti visited our family from Tehran for a couple of weeks. She is an incredible cook and she pulled out all of the stops for us, many times over, during the weeks she was in town. One of the lasting bits of culinary wisdom that she shared with me was that pink peppercorns are quite mild and floral in flavor, making them an excellent addition to desserts like this fresh and slightly spicy sorbet. The alcohol in this recipe helps the sorbet maintain a soft, scoopable texture straight from the freezer, but you can easily leave it out to make this recipe booze free.

1¼ cups (250g) granulated sugar

1 cup (240ml) water

2 tablespoons pink peppercorns

2 strips lemon zest, peeled with a vegetable peeler

12 ounces (340g) raspberries

1 tablespoon raspberry liqueur or vodka

Fresh raspberries, to serve (optional)

Prosecco, to serve (optional)

Combine the sugar, water, pink peppercorns, and lemon zest in a medium saucepan. Bring to a boil over high heat, stirring occasionally. Cook until all of the sugar is dissolved, then turn off the heat and let the mixture cool to room temperature.

Add the raspberries to the syrup and mash a few times with a potato masher or fork to break up the berries. Press the mixture through a fine-mesh sieve or food mill to remove the seeds. Stir in the raspberry liqueur or vodka, and chill the mixture thoroughly, at least 4 hours or up to overnight.

Freeze the mixture in an ice cream machine according to manufacturer's instructions. Transfer to a freezer-safe container, cover, and freeze until firm, at least 4 hours. Keeps for one week in the freezer.

Serve with fresh raspberries and a splash of Prosecco on top of each serving, if you are feeling festive.

FIGS

FIGS RIPEN AT THE END OF SUMMER AND SOMETIMES THROUGH EARLY FALL DEPENDING ON THE VARIETY. THEY COME IN MANY SHADES, SOME DEEP PURPLE WITH PINK OR BROWN INTERIORS AND SOME BRIGHT CHARTREUSE WITH MAGENTA CENTERS. LOOK FOR PLUMP AND SLIGHTLY SOFT FRUIT WITH SKIN SO DELICATE IT LOOKS LIKE IT MIGHT BURST, THEN ENJOY THEM QUICKLY. RIPE FIGS CAN BE STORED IN THE REFRIGERATOR FOR A DAY OR TWO, IN A SINGLE LAYER TO PREVENT DAMAGING THEIR TENDER SKINS AND MOLD GROWTH, BUT THEY WON'T LAST MUCH LONGER THAN THAT.

WINE-ROASTED FIGS WITH WHIPPED HONEYED RICOTTA

| SERVES 6 TO 8

FIGS

1 pound (450g) ripe
fresh figs

½ vanilla bean

2 tablespoons mild honey,
like clover or wildflower

½ cup (120ml) dry
red wine

1 bay leaf

1 tablespoon unsalted
butter

RICOTTA

½ vanilla bean, or
1 teaspoon vanilla extract
(page 235)

2 cups (470g) whole milk
ricotta

¼ cup (60ml) heavy cream

¼ cup (60ml) mild honey

Pinch salt

TO SERVE

Cacao nibs

Mild honey, like clover or
wildflower (optional)

*Sometimes I like to take a nod from my European friends and have
a cheese course for dessert. To make it a little bit special, I make
these wine-roasted figs with creamy whipped ricotta sweetened with
honey. This dessert can be served in shallow bowls with crunchy
cacao nibs on top, but for an even more elegant presentation, bake an
All-Purpose Tart Shell (page 232) or Chocolate Tart Shell (page 234),
fill the cooled shell with the whipped ricotta, and top with the figs just
before serving.*

Position a rack at the center of the oven and preheat to 375ºF (190ºC).

To roast the figs: Use the tip of a knife to slice the vanilla bean in half
lengthwise and scrape out the seeds; reserve the pod. Stem the figs and
slice half of them in half lengthwise (reserve the rest of the figs for later).
Put the fig halves in a small baking dish in a single layer. Whisk the
honey, wine, and vanilla seeds in a small bowl, then pour the mixture
over the figs. Tuck the vanilla pod and bay leaf in among the figs on the
baking sheet, then dot the tops of the figs with the butter. Slide the sheet
into the oven and bake, stirring occasionally, until the figs are soft and
the juices begin to caramelize, 20 to 25 minutes.

To make the whipped ricotta: Use the tip of a knife to slice the vanilla
bean in half lengthwise and scrape out the seeds; reserve the pod for
another use. Add the ricotta, cream, honey, vanilla bean seeds, and salt
to a bowl. Whip with an electric mixer or whisk until well-combined
and fluffy, about 2 minutes.

To serve: Slice the remaining figs into quarters. For each serving, spread
about ⅓ cup of the whipped ricotta in a shallow bowl, then top with a
mixture of the fresh quartered figs and the roasted fig halves. Spoon a
tablespoon or so of the wine syrup from the fig roasting pan over the top,
drizzle with honey, and sprinkle with cacao nibs. Serve immediately.

SOFT CHOCOLATE AND FIG CAKE

| MAKES ONE 8-INCH CAKE

This cake is part brownie, part fig-studded chocolate cake, and totally delicious. Be careful not to over bake it as it is best just a little soft and gooey in the middle. Serve warm, scooped from the pan into bowls or let it cool to room temperature and slice it into wedges.

¾ cup (95g)
all purpose flour

½ cup (50g) cocoa
powder

½ teaspoon baking
powder

½ teaspoon salt

1¼ cups (250g)
granulated sugar

½ cup (115g) unsalted
butter, melted and cooled
to room temperature

3 large eggs, at room
temperature

1 teaspoon vanilla extract
(page 235)

½ cup (85g) chopped
bittersweet chocolate

12 ounces (340g) fresh
figs, sliced into ¼-inch
(6mm) rounds

2 tablespoons
confectioners' sugar,
to serve

Unsweetened whipped
cream, to serve (optional)

Position a rack in the center of the oven and preheat to 350ºF (180ºC). Butter the bottom and sides of an 8-inch springform pan or cake pan. Line the bottom with parchment paper and butter that too. Dust the pan and paper with flour.

Sift the flour, cocoa powder, baking powder, and salt together in a bowl. In the bowl of a stand mixer on medium low, whisk the sugar into the butter, followed by the eggs and vanilla. Turn the mixer up to medium high and beat the mixture until it lightens in color and texture, about 2 minutes. Fold in the flour mixture, followed by the chopped chocolate.

Pour the batter into the pan, use an offset spatula to smooth the top, and arrange the sliced figs on top in a decorative pattern. Bake the cake until it is just set, but still wiggly in the center, 30 to 35 minutes. Cool the cake and slice it into wedges, or spoon the still-warm cake out of the pan into bowls. The center will remain slightly soft when cooled. Dust with confectioners' sugar and a dollop of unsweetened whipped cream just before serving.

fall

For all of summer's conspicuous abundance, fall's quiet bounty is just as wonderful. Maybe it's the Seattleite in me, but cool rainy mornings make September and October my favorite months of the year to wander the market. I take my time and move slowly through the stalls, usually eating one of the deliciously crisp new-crop apples that signal the change of season. I fill my bags with endless varieties of heirloom apples, pears, and squash until I can barely hoist them over my shoulders; and I make it my duty to drive to the Hudson Valley to sip cider, pick some of the tastiest apples in the country, and snip perfectly shaped clusters of deep-purple Concord grapes off of the vine. October also brings fuzzy green and yellow quince, which are rock hard and quite tannic when raw, but when poached in syrup, soften and release their lovely floral flavor. Quince may be a challenge to find, but seek them out if you can. They are worth the trouble. In a last showing of more delicate fruit, early fall also brings a second crop of raspberries along with persimmons and jewel-toned pomegranates that are perfect for bright and fresh-tasting desserts.

When you are at the market, make sure to choose apples and pears that are firm, so they can hold up to baking, but not so hard and unripe that they are dry and flavorless. When choosing apples, I like to pick varieties that are on the tart side: Mutsu, Pink Lady, McIntosh, Ginger Gold, Pippin, and Cortland are some of my favorite varieties. For pears, I stick to Bartlett, d'Anjou, Bosc, and a miniature variety called Seckel, which all hold up to cooking very well.

GRAPES

I ATE MY FIRST CONCORD GRAPE AT THE UNION
SQUARE FARMERS' MARKET SHORTLY AFTER
I MOVED TO NEW YORK, AND WAS IMMEDIATELY
HOOKED. CONCORDS ARE MUSKY AND SWEET,
SO CONCENTRATED IN FLAVOR THEY TASTE JAMMY
STRAIGHT FROM THE VINE. THEY ARE ALSO
UNDENIABLY BEAUTIFUL: DEEP PURPLE WITH A
LIGHT-COLORED BLOOM THAT GLOWS WHEN IT
CATCHES THE LIGHT JUST RIGHT. YOU MAY NOT
SEE CONCORD GRAPES AT YOUR LOCAL GROCERY
STORE, BUT A FARMERS' MARKET IS YOUR BEST
BET FOR FINDING CLUSTERS OF THESE DEEPLY
HUED AND FLAVORFUL GRAPES.

CONCORD GRAPE PIE WITH RYE CRUST

| MAKES ONE 9-INCH PIE

1 recipe Rye Pie Crust
(see rye variation on
All-Butter Pie Crust,
page 228)

FILLING

2 pounds (900g) Concord
grapes, stemmed

1 small apple

⅔ cup (135g)
granulated sugar

¼ cup (30g) cornstarch

2 tablespoons orange
juice

1 teaspoon orange zest

½ teaspoon ground
cinnamon

¼ teaspoon freshly
grated nutmeg

Pinch salt

TOPPING

1 large egg, lightly beaten
for egg wash

1 tablespoon
turbinado sugar

TO SERVE

Ice cream or lightly
sweetened whipped
cream

You may get a few sideways glances from your friends when you announce that you've made them a grape pie, but rest assured those glances will turn into contented smiles upon first bite of this sweet, tart, and lightly spiced pie. The addition of a chopped apple gives the filling a little bit of texture, so choose a firm variety that can stand up to baking, like Granny Smith or Ginger Gold. I like to make this pie with my favorite rye crust because of the wholesome and slightly milky flavor it gets from the rye flour. Make sure to let the pie cool to room temperature before slicing or you will have a juicy mess on your hands.

To make the filling: Pinch each grape between your thumb and index finger to slip off their skins. Reserve the skins in a large bowl and put the pulp in a saucepan. Cook the pulp over medium heat, stirring occasionally, until the grape seeds begin to separate from the flesh, 8 to 10 minutes.

Pass the mixture through a food mill or strain through a fine-mesh sieve into the bowl with the skins, pressing the solids through the sieve with the back of a spoon until only the seeds are left in the sieve. Discard the seeds and set the mixture aside to cool while you prepare the rest of the filling.

Peel, core, and chop the apple into ¼-inch pieces. In a small bowl, whisk the sugar, cornstarch, orange juice and zest, spices, and salt together, then add this to the grape mixture along with the chopped apple. Stir until well combined.

On a lightly floured surface, roll out one piece of the pie dough into a roughly 12-inch circle about ⅛ to ¼ inch thick. Place it in a 9-inch pie pan. Roll out the other piece of dough into an 11-inch circle about ⅛ to ¼ inch thick.

CONTINUED

CONCORD GRAPE PIE WITH RYE CRUST, CONTINUED

Fill the pie shell with the prepared filling and top with the second crust. Trim the edges so they are even, then fold and crimp the edges together. Slide the whole pie into the freezer until the crust is very firm, about 15 minutes.

While the pie is chilling, position a rack in the lower third of the oven and preheat to 400ºF (200ºC). Line a baking sheet with parchment paper. When you are ready to bake the pie, place it on the baking sheet to catch any drips. Brush the crust with the egg wash, sprinkle with the turbinado sugar, and cut a few vents in the top.

Bake the pie until it is deep golden brown and the juices are bubbling, 45 to 55 minutes. If the crust begins to burn before the filling bubbles, tent it with aluminum foil. Cool the pie to room temperature before slicing. Serve with vanilla ice cream or a dollop of lightly sweetened whipped cream.

CONCORD GRAPE AND PLUM BUTTER

| MAKES ABOUT 2 PINTS (900G)

Concord grapes taste like the pure essence of grape. They are strong and musky and quite sweet, like Welch's grape juice times one hundred. Here, their flavor is mellowed with Italian plums and a small amount of sweet vanilla and spicy cinnamon. I like my fruit preserves to be quite simple in flavor so I can get the most use out of them, but if you like strongly spiced jams or fruit butters, feel free use up to 1 tablespoon of cinnamon. Make sure to cook this fruit butter until it spits and spatters with big lazy bubbles. Any less than that and you'll have more of a grape and plum sauce on your hands—which isn't all that bad over yogurt really.

1½ pounds (680g) Concord grapes, stemmed

1 pound (450g) Italian plums, pitted and coarsely chopped

1 medium apple, peeled, cored, and coarsely chopped

2¾ cups plus 2 tablespoons (565g) granulated sugar

1 vanilla bean, or 2 teaspoons vanilla extract (page 235)

1 teaspoon ground cinnamon

Juice of 1 lemon (about 3 tablespoons)

2 pint (480ml) or 4 half-pint (240ml) canning jars

Combine the grapes, plums, apple, and sugar in a large, heavy-bottomed pot. Cook over medium high heat, stirring occasionally, until the sugar has dissolved and the fruit has softened completely and released its juices, 10 to 15 minutes.

Working carefully, and in batches if necessary, pass the mixture through a food mill set over a large bowl. Alternately, use some elbow grease and pass the mixture through a fine mesh sieve, pressing it through with a wooden spoon. Discard the leftover seeds and skins. Use the tip of a knife to split the vanilla bean lengthwise and scrape out the seeds.

Return the fruit puree to the pot on the stove and add the cinnamon, vanilla seeds and pod, and lemon juice. Cook the mixture over medium high heat, stirring often, until the fruit butter is very thick and bubbles lazily in the pot, 25 to 35 minutes. Keep a close eye on the pot and stir more often later in the cooking process so the bottom doesn't scorch.

When the fruit butter has thickened, carefully remove the vanilla pod, rinse it, and save it for another use. Ladle the fruit butter into clean, sterilized canning jars, leaving ¼ inch of headspace. Wipe the rims with a clean towel and screw on the lids tightly. Let the jars cool to room temperature, then store them in the fridge. The jars will keep, refrigerated, for up to one month.

PERSIMMONS AND POMEGRANATES

PERSIMMONS COME IN TWO COMMONLY KNOWN VARIETIES: SHORT AND SQUAT FUYUS AND ACORN-SHAPED HACHIYAS. FUYUS CAN BE PEELED, SLICED, AND ENJOYED WHEN THEY ARE STILL SLIGHTLY FIRM. HACHIYAS ARE QUITE ASTRINGENT AND ARE BEST ENJOYED WHEN THEY ARE SO RIPE THAT THEY ARE SOFT AND THEIR SKIN IS STARTING TO GO TRANSLUCENT. THEIR FLESH IS BEST USED AS A PUREE. POMEGRANATES ARE A STAPLE IN MOST MIDDLE EASTERN KITCHENS, AND I LOVE USING THEIR TART AND CRUNCHY SEEDS TO GARNISH ALL SORTS OF DESSERTS. POMEGRANATE MOLASSES, WITH ITS SIMILAR SWEET-TART FLAVOR PROFILE IS ALSO DELICIOUS IN BOTH SWEET AND SAVORY DISHES WHEN FRESH POMEGRANATES ARE NOT AVAILABLE.

JEWELED PAVLOVAS WITH CRANBERRY CURD

| MAKES 8 INDIVIDUAL PAVLOVAS

MERINGUES

4 large egg whites

1½ teaspoons cornstarch

1 cup (200g) superfine sugar

¼ teaspoon salt

⅛ teaspoon cream of tartar

1 teaspoon vanilla extract (page 235)

1 teaspoon white vinegar

CRANBERRY CURD

¾ cup (180ml) 100 percent Unsweetened Cranberry Juice (page 240)

3 large eggs

1 large egg yolk

⅔ cup (135g) granulated sugar

Pinch salt

¾ cup (170g) cold unsalted butter, cut into 12 equal pieces

TO SERVE

1 cup (240ml) heavy cream, whipped to soft peaks

1½ cups pomegranate seeds (from about 2 pomegranates)

6 Fuyu persimmons, peeled and cut into six wedges each

These jeweled pavlovas—crisp meringue shells topped with rosy pink cranberry curd, red pomegranate arils, and bright orange persimmon slices—make for an elegant, fall-hued dessert. Use short and squat Fuyu persimmons rather than the acorn-shaped Hachiya variety here. Fuyus are ripe when they give just slightly when pressed with your fingertips.

Position two racks in the center and top third of the oven and preheat to 225ºF (110ºC). Line two baking sheets with parchment paper.

To make the meringues: Stir the cornstarch and sugar together in a small bowl. In the bowl of a stand mixer fitted with the whisk attachment or with a handheld electric mixer in a large bowl, beat the egg whites, salt, and cream of tartar on medium high speed until soft peaks form. Turn the mixer up to high and with the mixer running, slowly add the sugar mixture about one tablespoon at a time until you have added all of it and the egg whites are stiff and glossy, about 7 minutes. Add the vanilla and vinegar and mix for 30 more seconds.

Dollop the meringue onto the baking sheets in eight even 3-inch mounds at least 2 inches apart (4 per baking sheet). Use a spoon to make a small indent in the center of each mound. Bake the meringues for 1 to 1½ hours, rotating the pans from top to bottom and front to back halfway through, or until the outside looks dry and slightly creamy in color. Turn off the oven and prop the door ajar with a wooden spoon. Let the meringues cool completely in the oven. They should feel firm and crackly when you press them, but will be soft and marshmallowy in the center. When cooled, they should easily peel off of the parchment paper.

CONTINUED

To make the cranberry curd: Combine the cranberry juice, eggs, egg yolk, sugar, and salt in a nonreactive saucepan. Cook the mixture over medium low heat, whisking constantly, until it is very thick and reaches 180°F (82°C) on a candy thermometer. If you do not have a candy thermometer, cook the mixture until it is very thick and a whisk leaves a trail through the curd, about 10 minutes. Remove from the heat and let cool, stirring occasionally to release the heat, for about 10 minutes.

When the cranberry mixture has cooled slightly, pour it into a blender. With the blender running, add the butter one piece at a time, blending after each addition. The cream will thicken slightly and turn a lovely shade of light coral pink. Chill the curd in the refrigerator completely before assembling the pavlovas.

To assemble: Add a dollop of whipped cream to each meringue, followed by a dollop of the chilled cranberry curd. Scatter the persimmon wedges and pomegranate seeds evenly over the tops and serve immediately.

PERSIMMON SORBET WITH GINGER AND VANILLA

| MAKES ABOUT 3 CUPS (680G)

A generous amount of fresh grated ginger gives this naturally sweet and pleasantly creamy persimmon sorbet some warmth and spice. Acorn-shaped Hachiya persimmons are the best variety for this sorbet, but you must make sure they are very, very ripe—they will be very soft with almost translucent skin when ready.

1 vanilla bean

½ cup (100g) sugar

½ cup (120ml) water

1 tablespoon peeled and grated fresh ginger

5 large, extremely ripe Hachiya persimmons

2 tablespoons lemon juice

¼ teaspoon salt

Use the tip of a knife to split the vanilla bean in half lengthwise and scrape out the seeds. Combine the sugar, water, vanilla seeds and pod, and ginger in a saucepan set over medium heat. Cook the mixture until the sugar dissolves, then turn off the heat and let it infuse for 15 minutes. Remove the vanilla bean from the syrup and use the tip of a knife to scrape any remaining seeds into the syrup. Rinse the pod and save it for another use.

Cut the tops off the persimmons and scoop the flesh (the persimmons may or may not have a couple of black seeds, if they do, remove them before blending) into a food processor or blender and process until very smooth. Pass the mixture through a fine mesh sieve, pressing on the solids with a wooden spoon, and measure out 2 cups of puree.

Whisk the cooled syrup, persimmon puree, lemon juice, and salt together in a bowl until well combined. Chill the mixture until very cold, at least 4 hours or overnight.

Freeze the chilled mixture in an ice cream machine according to manufacturer's instructions. Serve immediately as soft serve, or spoon the sorbet into a freezer-safe container, cover, and freeze until firm, about 4 hours. This sorbet will keep in the freezer for up to one week.

APPLES

APPLES ARE AVAILABLE YEAR-ROUND, BUT THEY
ARE TRULY AT THEIR BEST IN THE FALL, FRESH FROM
THE ORCHARD INSTEAD OF FROM COLD STORAGE.
IN RECENT YEARS, I HAVE BEEN DELIGHTED TO FIND
THAT FARMERS ARE GROWING AND SELLING MORE
HEIRLOOM APPLE VARIETIES PRIZED FOR THEIR
WONDERFULLY NUANCED FLAVORS, RATHER THAN
FOR PICTURE-PERFECT APPEARANCES. THIS YEAR,
SKIP THE GRANNY SMITH AND RED DELICIOUS
AND SEEK OUT HEIRLOOM VARIETIES LIKE GOLDEN
RUSSET, COX'S ORANGE PIPPIN, AND BALDWIN FOR
YOUR FALL BAKING. I AM ALSO PARTIAL TO MUTSU,
GINGER GOLD, AND MACOUN APPLES, WHICH MAY
BE EASIER TO FIND.

MARIE-DANIELLE'S APPLE TART

| MAKES ONE 10 BY 15-INCH TART

I learned how to make this supremely simple and surprisingly tasty tart from my friend Amelie, who in turn learned how to make it from her mother, Marie-Danielle. I know the lineage goes back further than that, but I associate it with those two lovely women, so Marie-Danielle gets the credit here. I've modified the recipe slightly to use homemade spelt puff pastry instead of traditional puff pastry, for its wholesome flavor and exceptionally light texture. If you are pinched for time, store-bought puff pastry makes a fine substitute. Use Dufour or another brand made with all butter instead of vegetable shortening for the tastiest results. Marie-Danielle and Amelie like to use Granny Smith and Gala apples, but any firm, tart apples will work wonderfully.

⅓ recipe (450g) Spelt Quick Puff Pastry (page 231)

4 large tart baking apples, about 2 pounds (900g)

2 tablespoons all purpose flour

6 tablespoons (75g) Vanilla Sugar (page 235) or granulated sugar

Pinch salt

1 large egg, lightly beaten for egg wash

1 tablespoon turbinado sugar

Crème Fraîche (page 229) or lightly sweetened whipped cream, to serve

Line a baking sheet with parchment paper. Peel, core, and slice the apples into ⅛-inch slices. On a lightly floured surface, roll the puff pastry into a 10 by 15-inch rectangle. Trim the edges so they are more or less straight and even. Transfer the pastry to the baking sheet and sprinkle the flour and 2 tablespoons of granulated sugar over the top, leaving a 1-inch border around the edges. Arrange the apple slices on top of the dough so the edges slightly overlap, while leaving a 1-inch border around the edges. Sprinkle the remaining granulated sugar and a pinch of salt over the apples. Fold the edges of the dough up and over the apples and press gently to seal at the corners. Pop the baking sheet into the freezer for about 15 minutes, or until the dough is firm.

Position a rack in the center of the oven and preheat to 425°F (220°C). When you are ready to bake, brush the dough with egg wash and sprinkle with turbinado sugar.

Bake the tart, turning the pan halfway through baking until the apples are soft and browning around the edges and the pastry is deep golden brown, 30 to 40 minutes. Cut into slices and serve with whipped cream or crème fraîche. This tart is best the day it's made, although it makes a fine breakfast the next morning.

CARAMELIZED APPLE FRITTERS

| MAKES ABOUT 12 FRITTERS

DOUGH

1 teaspoon active
dry yeast

½ cup (120ml) whole milk,
warmed to 110°F (43°C)

2 tablespoons granulated
sugar

2 tablespoons unsalted
butter, melted and cooled

1 large egg, at room
temperature

1 teaspoon vanilla extract
(page 235)

1¾ cups (220g) all
purpose flour, plus more
as needed

½ teaspoon salt

¼ teaspoon ground
cinnamon

¼ teaspoon freshly
grated nutmeg

APPLES

2 firm baking apples such
as Granny Smith, Mutsu,
or Ginger Gold

3 tablespoons sugar

1 tablespoon water

2 teaspoons lemon juice

1 tablespoon unsalted
butter

½ teaspoon ground
cinnamon

Pinch salt

INGREDIENTS CONTINUED

Apple fritters are the kind of dessert that won't turn any heads with their beauty. However, their humble exterior gives way to the perfect combination of gently spiced yeast dough with little pockets of caramelized apples and a thin layer of sweet vanilla and cardamom-scented glaze.

To make the dough: In a large bowl, or the bowl of a stand mixer fitted with the paddle attachment, stir the yeast into the milk. Let sit until the yeast is foamy, about 5 minutes. Whisk the sugar, butter, egg, and vanilla together in a small bowl, then whisk the mixture into the foamy yeast.

Add the flour, salt, and spices to the mixer bowl and stir the dough on low speed with the paddle attachment until all of the flour is moistened. Switch to the dough hook and mix for 4 more minutes. The dough will be very soft and will stick to the bottom of the bowl, but if it seems more like batter than dough, add more flour a couple of tablespoons at time. Transfer the dough to an oiled bowl and cover with plastic wrap. Let the dough rest in a draft-free spot until almost doubled in size, about 1 hour. While the dough is rising, prepare the apples.

To make the apples: Peel, core, and dice the apples into ¼-inch pieces. Combine the sugar and 1 tablespoon of water in an 8-inch skillet and cook over medium high heat, swirling the pan occasionally until the sugar melts and turns a deep amber color. Don't walk away from the pan while you are caramelizing the sugar. It will go from perfectly amber to burned in mere seconds. Take the pan off of the heat and carefully add the apples and lemon juice to the hot caramel and stir to combine. Return the pan to the heat. The sugar may seize up a bit, but keep stirring, the apples will release their juices and the sugar will re-melt.

CONTINUED

GLAZE

2 cups (200g)
confectioners' sugar

¼ cup (60ml) whole milk

½ teaspoon vanilla
extract (page 235)

¼ teaspoon ground
cardamom

Pinch salt

TO FRY

Vegetable oil

Cook until the apples are soft, and golden from the caramel, and the pan is almost dry, 5 to 7 minutes. Stir in the butter, cinnamon, and salt. Set the mixture aside to cool.

To assemble the fritters: Pat the dough out onto a well-floured surface into a rectangle about ½ inch thick, flouring the surface as necessary. Spread half of the apple mixture over the top of the dough, leaving a 1-inch border all around the edges, and fold the dough into thirds, like a letter. Pat the folded dough into a rectangle about 1 inch thick, spread the rest of the apples on top, and fold into thirds again.

Again, pat the dough into a rectangle about 1 inch thick on a well-floured surface, then use a bench scraper or pizza cutter to cut the dough into roughly 24 (2-inch) squares. The squares don't have to be perfect. Use well floured hands (or spray your hands with a bit of cooking spray) to form the dough into about 12 mounds. Try your best to tuck all of the apples into the dough, but don't worry if some just don't want to stay put. Gently flatten the mounds with the palm of your hand and let the dough rest for about 15 minutes.

Meanwhile, make the glaze by whisking the confectioners' sugar, milk, vanilla, cardamom, and salt together in a bowl. Set aside.

To fry the fritters: Add oil to a Dutch oven or deep-sided skillet to a depth of at least 3 inches. Heat the oil over medium heat until it reaches 365ºF (185ºC) on a candy thermometer. While the oil is heating, line a baking sheet with paper towels and place a cooling rack on top.

Carefully place the mounds of dough in the hot oil one at a time, making sure to not crowd the pan. Keep an eye on the temperature of the oil; you may have to raise or lower the heat under the pan to keep the oil at a consistent temperature, which is the secret to successful deep-frying. Fry the fritters until they are deep golden brown, about 90 seconds, then use a spatula or spider strainer to carefully flip them. Cook on the other side for about 90 seconds or until deep golden brown and cooked through. You may lose some of the apples in the frying oil; just make sure to remove them from the oil along with each batch of fritters. Remove the fritters to the rack and fry the next batch of dough mounds. When each batch is cool enough to touch, dip each fritter in the glaze and let the excess drip off. Set the fritters on the rack glaze side up and let them sit until the glaze is no longer sticky. Serve warm or at room temperature. These fritters are best the day they are made.

CAMPFIRE CRISP

| MAKES ONE 9 BY 13-INCH CRISP

Crisp Topping,
whole wheat variation
(page 230)

FILLING

2½ pounds (1125g) firm
baking apples

1 pound (450g) Italian
plums

1 heaping cup (170g)
Concord grapes

1 vanilla bean, or
2 teaspoons vanilla
extract (page 235)

1 teaspoon orange zest

1 teaspoon lemon zest

⅓ cup (65g)
granulated sugar

¼ cup (32g)
all purpose flour

1 teaspoon ground
cinnamon

Pinch salt

TO SERVE

Ice cream or lightly
sweetened whipped
cream (optional)

The first time I made a crisp with this combination of fruit I was on the tail end of a weekend in the mountains of upstate New York, and was on a mission to use up all of our leftover fruit before heading back to the city. I mixed everything in a Dutch oven, tucked the pot into the hot embers of our campfire, crossed my fingers, and hoped the thing wouldn't turn into a burned mess—it didn't, thank goodness. This version is baked in a more traditional manner, but the same flavors are there, warm and comforting as always.

Position a rack in the center of the oven and preheat to 375ºF (190ºC).

Use the tip of a knife to slice the vanilla bean in half lengthwise and scrape out the seeds; reserve the pod for another use. In a large bowl, rub the vanilla seeds, orange zest, and lemon zest into the sugar with your fingertips. Stir in the flour, cinnamon, and salt.

Peel, core, and chop the apples into ½-inch pieces. Pit the plums and chop them into similar-size pieces. Seed the grapes by slicing them in half and pushing the seeds out with your fingertips. Add the fruit to the bowl with the sugar mixture and toss gently to combine.

Pour the fruit and all of its juices into a 9 by 13-inch or 3 quart baking dish. Scatter the crisp topping evenly over the fruit. Bake until the fruit is bubbling and the topping is golden brown, 30 to 40 minutes. Serve warm with ice cream or whipped cream if desired.

SEASONAL VARIATIONS: If you're making this crisp later into the fall or winter and the plums and grapes aren't available, substitute a 12-ounce (340g) bag of cranberries for them and increase the sugar by 2 tablespoons.

PEARS

UNLIKE MANY FRUITS, PEARS ONLY FULLY RIPEN OFF THE BRANCH. LOOK FOR FIRM PEARS WITH UNBLEMISHED SKINS AND STORE THEM AT ROOM TEMPERATURE FOR A FEW DAYS BEFORE USING. THEY ARE RIPE WHEN THEY YIELD JUST SLIGHTLY WHEN PRESSED NEAR THEIR STEMS. PEARS THAT ARE JUST RIPE ARE BEST FOR BAKING, SOFT AND JUICY PEARS SHOULD BE SAVED FOR EATING OUT OF HAND OR FOR SAUCE. SOME VARIETIES THAT WORK WELL FOR BAKING ARE BARTLETTS, BOSCS, AND D'ANJOUS. I ALSO LIKE MINIATURE SECKEL PEARS, BUT THEY CAN BE MORE DIFFICULT TO FIND.

A PEAR-PACKED CHESTNUT CAKE

| MAKES ONE 9-INCH CAKE

Roasted chestnuts have a rich nutty flavor that is pleasantly lightened with bright sweet pears in this cake. Choose ripe but firm pears for this cake: d'Anjou or Bosc pears are both nice choices. This cake is sweet, dense, and nutty, but to make it a bit more luxurious, fold in ⅓ cup (60g) of chopped bittersweet chocolate when you fold in the pears and walnuts.

½ cup (50g) chopped walnuts

3 medium-size pears (about 1 pound/450g)

1¼ cups (155g) all purpose flour

1 teaspoon baking powder

¾ teaspoon salt

1 (5-ounce/150g) package shelled roasted chestnuts

1 cup (200g) sugar

¾ cup (170g) unsalted butter, softened

4 large eggs, at room temperature

2 teaspoons vanilla extract (page 235)

1 tablespoon confectioners' sugar

Position a rack in the center of the oven and preheat to 350ºF (180ºC). Butter and flour a 9-inch cake pan.

Arrange the walnuts in a single layer on a baking sheet. Toast in the oven until they are light brown and fragrant, about 10 minutes. Let the nuts cool while you prepare the rest of the cake.

Peel, core, and chop the pears into ½-inch pieces. Whisk the flour, baking powder, and salt together in a small bowl.

In the bowl of a stand mixer fitted with the paddle attachment, or in a large bowl, combine the chestnuts and sugar. Mix on low speed until the chestnuts have broken up into a coarse meal. Add the butter, turn the mixer up to medium high and cream the mixture until light and fluffy, about 5 minutes. Add the eggs one at a time, mixing for 30 seconds and scraping down to the bottom of the bowl in between each addition. Add the vanilla extract.

Use a rubber spatula to fold in the flour mixture until just combined, then fold in the pears and walnuts. The batter will be quite thick. Spoon the batter into the prepared pan, and spread it out evenly with an offset spatula. Tap the pan gently on the counter to help the batter settle in the pan.

Bake until a toothpick inserted into the center of the cake comes out clean and the edges are golden brown, 40 to 50 minutes. Let the cake cool in the pan for 15 minutes, then remove to a rack to cool completely. Dust with confectioners' sugar just before serving. Leftovers can be stored at room temperature in an airtight container for two days.

PEAR PIE WITH CRÈME FRAÎCHE CARAMEL

| MAKES ONE 9-INCH PIE

I don't know why more people aren't making pear pies. After making this one, loaded with sweet and spiced pears, I have decided that I might even like them better than traditional apple. The key to a successful pear pie is to choose pears that are ripe but still quite firm so that the filling has a bit of texture after baking. Keep those extra juicy ones to snack on. The spices in this pie are muted and subtle to really let the flavor of the pears shine, and as for the sauce—well what isn't better with a bit of caramel?

1 recipe (720g) All-Butter Pie Crust (page 228)

2½ pounds (1125g) ripe but firm pears

¼ cup (50g) granulated sugar

¼ cup (32g) all purpose flour

½ teaspoon ground cinnamon

¼ teaspoon freshly grated nutmeg

¼ teaspoon ground allspice

Juice of ½ lemon (about 4 teaspoons)

½ cup (115ml) Crème Fraîche Caramel Sauce (page 229)

1 large egg, lightly beaten for egg wash

1 tablespoon turbinado sugar

Position a rack in the lower third of the oven and preheat to 425ºF (220ºC).

On a lightly floured surface, roll out one piece of the pie dough into a roughly 12-inch circle about ⅛ to ¼-inch thick. Place it into a 9-inch pie pan and store in the refrigerator while you prepare the rest of the pie.

To make a lattice top: Roll out the other piece of dough into a 12-inch circle about ⅛ to ¼-inch thick, and cut it into 2-inch-wide strips. Transfer the strips to a baking sheet and refrigerate while you prepare the filling.

Peel and core the pears and slice them into ¼-inch slices. Put them in a large bowl along with the sugar, flour, spices, and lemon juice and stir gently to combine.

Add half of the pears to the pie shell, drizzle the caramel sauce over the top, then add the remaining pears. Lay out half of the prepared dough strips evenly spaced on top of the filling. Fold every other strip back, then place a dough strip in the center. Unfold the strips you folded back over the center strip. Take the parallel strips that are underneath the center strip and

CONTINUED

fold every other one back over the center strip. Lay down another strip next to the center strip, leaving a little space between. Unfold the parallel strips over the second strip. Repeat until all of the dough strips have been used.

Trim off the excess lattice and fold the edges of the bottom crust up and over the lattice strips. Crimp the edges together. Slide the whole pie into the freezer until the crust is very firm, about 15 minutes, before baking.

When you are ready to bake the pie, place it on a baking sheet to catch any drips. Beat the egg, then brush the top of the pie with the egg wash and sprinkle with the turbinado sugar.

Bake the pie until it is deep golden brown and the juices are bubbling, 45 to 55 minutes. If the crust begins to burn before the filling bubbles, tent it with aluminum foil. Cool slightly before serving. This pie is best the day it's made.

QUINCE

EVERY OCTOBER, MY PARENTS SEND ME A LOAD OF GNARLY QUINCE FROM A FRIEND'S TREE IN SEATTLE. THEY ARRIVE IN A BEAT-UP FLAT-RATE POST OFFICE BOX, EACH QUINCE LOVINGLY CUSHIONED WITH NEWSPAPER IN AN ATTEMPT TO PROTECT THEM FROM THE INEVITABLE BRUISING THAT OCCURS IN TRANSIT. I LET THEIR SWEET, FLORAL SCENT PERFUME MY APARTMENT FOR A FEW DAYS BEFORE TURNING THE QUINCE INTO CAKES AND TARTS THAT HIGHLIGHT THEIR UNIQUE FLAVOR. QUINCE RANGE FROM YELLOW TO GREEN IN COLOR AND OFTEN HAVE A THIN LAYER OF FUZZ ON THE OUTSIDE, DEPENDING ON THE VARIETY AND WHEN DURING THE SEASON THEY ARE HARVESTED.

GINGER QUINCE UPSIDE-DOWN CAKE

| MAKES ONE 9-INCH CAKE

TOPPING

4 tablespoons (55g) unsalted butter

½ cup (100g) firmly packed dark brown sugar

Pinch salt

3–4 Poached Quince (page 237), cut into ¼-inch slices, poaching liquid reserved

CAKE

1½ cups (190g) all purpose flour

¾ teaspoon baking soda

¾ teaspoon baking powder

¾ teaspoon salt

1 tablespoon ground ginger

1 teaspoon ground cinnamon

¼ teaspoon ground cloves

½ cup (115g) unsalted butter, softened

⅓ cup (70g) firmly packed dark brown sugar

1 tablespoon peeled and finely grated fresh ginger

2 large eggs, at room temperature

INGREDIENTS CONTINUED

Fragrant poached quince slices are a pleasantly sweet addition to this spicy ginger cake. Top a slice of cake with ice cream for an indulgent dessert or have a thin slice with a cup of tea for an afternoon treat. If you can't find quinces where you live, sliced apples, pears, or even Fuyu persimmons make a fine substitute.

Position a rack in the center of the oven and preheat to 350ºF (175ºC). Butter a 9-inch round baking pan with sides at least 2 inches tall. Line the pan with a round of parchment paper and butter that, too. Dust the pan and paper with flour.

To make the topping: In a small saucepan or skillet, combine the butter, brown sugar, and salt. Cook over medium heat for about 1 minute, whisking occasionally, until the sugar melts into the butter. Pour the mixture into the bottom of the prepared pan, then arrange the quince slices on top in concentric circles making sure that the bottom of the pan is completely covered with quince slices. Put the pan aside while you prepare the cake batter.

To make the cake: Whisk the flour, baking soda, baking powder, salt, and spices together.

In a stand mixer fitted with the paddle attachment, or in a bowl using an electric mixer, cream the butter and sugar together until very light and fluffy, about 5 minutes. Add the grated fresh ginger and mix for 1 more minute. Scrape down the bowl and add the eggs one at a time, mixing for 30 seconds after each addition. With the mixer on low speed, slowly pour in the molasses and mix for 1 more minute. Stop the mixer to scrape down the sides of the bowl. The batter may look broken or curdled at this point, but don't worry; once the flour and buttermilk are added, it will come back together.

CONTINUED

GINGER QUINCE UPSIDE-DOWN CAKE, CONTINUED

⅓ cup (80ml) unsulfured molasses

¾ cup (180ml) buttermilk, at room temperature

TO SERVE

3 tablespoons quince poaching liquid
(see page 237)

Ice cream or lightly sweetened whipped cream

With the mixer on low speed, alternately add the flour mixture and the buttermilk to the batter in three additions. Finish mixing the batter by hand with a rubber spatula, making sure to scrape the bottom and sides of the bowl. Carefully pour the batter into the prepared pan, tap the pan gently on the counter to release any air bubbles, and smooth the top with an offset spatula.

Bake until lightly golden brown and a toothpick inserted in the center of the cake comes out clean, 40 to 45 minutes. Let the cake cool in the pan for about 10 minutes, then invert onto a plate and gently peel away the parchment paper. Replace any quince slices that have stuck to the paper.

To serve: Brush the quince poaching liquid over the quince slices and cake. Serve the cake warm or room temperature with a bit of ice cream or lightly sweetened whipped cream. Store leftover cake in an airtight container at room temperature for up to two days.

QUINCE AND PISTACHIO FRANGIPANE TARTLETS

| MAKES SIX 4-INCH TARTLETS

Frangipane is a paste usually made from ground almonds, sugar, and eggs and is used in everything from croissants to bostock to tarts like these. In these tartlets, I have swapped in pistachios and quince poached with fragrant vanilla and citrus for a Middle Eastern twist on the classic pear and frangipane tart. The result is both visually striking and extremely tasty.

1 recipe All-Purpose Tart Shell (page 232), divided among six 4-inch tartlet pans and fully baked

2 Poached Quince (page 237)

PISTACHIO FRANGIPANE

6 tablespoons (85g) unsalted butter, softened

½ cup (100g) granulated sugar

1 cup (130g) shelled raw pistachios

1 large egg plus 1 large egg white

1 teaspoon vanilla extract (page 235)

¼ teaspoon almond extract

1 tablespoon all purpose flour

½ teaspoon salt

TO SERVE

1 tablespoon confectioners' sugar

Position a rack in the center of the oven and preheat to 350°F (180°C). Place the prebaked tart shells, still in their pans, on a baking sheet. Slice the quince into ¼-inch (6mm) slices; you will want about 24 slices, or 4 per tartlet.

To make the frangipane: Grind the pistachios and the sugar together in a food processor fitted with the steel blade until they resemble coarse sand. Pulse in the butter followed by the egg and egg white. Add the vanilla and almond extracts. Pulse in the flour and salt. Remove the blade and use a spatula to scrape the bottom and sides of the food processor to ensure that the frangipane is evenly mixed.

Divide the frangipane among the baked tartlet shells, leaving a little room at the top for the quince. You may have a little bit of extra frangipane. Lay the quince slices over the frangipane in a slightly overlapping single layer in a decorative pattern. Bake the tartlets until the frangipane is puffy and golden, 25 to 30 minutes. Let the tartlets cool completely, then dust with the confectioners' sugar just before serving. These tarts are best on the day they are made, but they will keep in the fridge in an airtight container for up to three days.

SQUASH AND PUMPKINS

SQUASH AND PUMPKINS ARE CONSIDERED
BY MANY TO BE VEGETABLES, BUT THEY ARE
BOTANICALLY CLASSIFIED AS FRUIT. THOUGH THEY
ARE WONDERFUL IN BOTH SAVORY AND SWEET
PREPARATIONS, I THINK THEY ESPECIALLY SHINE
WHEN THEY ARE ROASTED AND COMBINED WITH
TRADITIONALLY SWEET SPICES LIKE CINNAMON
AND NUTMEG. HARD-SKINNED SQUASH LIKE
BUTTERNUT, RED KURI, AND KABOCHA, ALONG
WITH SOME PUMPKIN VARIETIES LIKE WINTER
LUXURY AND SUGAR PUMPKINS, ALL MAKE
SMOOTH, SLIGHTLY SWEET PUREE.

BUTTERNUT SQUASH TEA CAKE

| MAKES TWO 9 BY 5-INCH LOAVES, OR 6 TO 8 SMALLER LOAVES

The heavy dose of nuts and seeds paired with coconut oil lend this cake a wholesome and nutty texture and flavor. Make sure that the eggs and buttermilk are at room temperature to avoid making the coconut oil seize in the batter.

½ cup (50g) walnuts

½ cup (50g) pecans

¾ cup (95g) pumpkin seeds

2½ cups (315g) all purpose flour

1 cup (125g) whole wheat pastry flour

2 teaspoons baking soda

2 teaspoons baking powder

1½ teaspoons salt

2 teaspoons ground cinnamon

½ teaspoon freshly grated nutmeg

1 cup (240ml) coconut oil, melted and cooled

1 cup (200g) firmly packed light brown sugar

1 cup (200g) granulated sugar

2 cups (450g) Roasted Winter Squash Puree (page 238)

4 large eggs, at room temperature

¾ cup (180ml) buttermilk, at room temperature

Position a rack in the center of the oven and preheat the oven to 375°F (190°C).

Spread the walnuts, pecans, and pumpkin seeds on a baking sheet in an even layer and bake for 10 to 15 minutes, or until they are nicely toasted and fragrant. Let the nuts cool, then chop them into medium-fine pieces.

Turn the oven down to 325°F (160°C) and butter and flour two 9 by 5 inch loaf pans or 6 to 8 mini loaf pans.

Whisk the flours, baking soda, baking powder, salt, and spices together. Stir in the chopped nuts and seeds, reserving a few tablespoons of nuts and seeds to sprinkle over the tops of the loaves.

In the bowl of a stand mixer fitted with the paddle attachment, combine the oil and sugars. Mix on medium high until well combined, about 2 minutes. Scrape down the sides of the bowl, add the squash puree, and continue to mix on medium speed for another 2 minutes. Add the eggs one at a time, mixing for 30 seconds after each addition.

With the mixer on low speed, alternately add the flour mixture and the buttermilk to the batter in three additions, mixing until just combined. Finish mixing the batter by hand with a rubber spatula.

Pour the batter into the prepared pans and smooth the tops. Tap the pans gently on the counter to release any air bubbles, then sprinkle with the reserved nuts and seeds. Bake large loaves for 50 to 60 minutes, smaller loaves for 25 to 35 minutes. They are done when a cake tester inserted into the center comes out clean. Cool the loaves for 20 minutes before unmolding. Store loaves in an airtight container at room temperature for up to four days.

CARAMEL-SWIRLED ROASTED SQUASH ICE CREAM

| MAKES ABOUT 1 QUART (900G)

Unlike most pumpkin and squash desserts, this ice cream is barely spiced, with just a hint of cinnamon. Instead, the sweet, roasted squash is enhanced with a generous swirl of caramel sauce and a splash of rum, which not only adds flavor, but helps the ice cream keep a soft and smooth texture straight from the freezer. Make sure to give the caramel sauce time to chill before churning the ice cream, as you want it to be close to room temperature when you drizzle it into the churned ice cream to avoid making a melty mess.

5 egg yolks

1½ cups (360ml) heavy cream

1 cup (240ml) milk

1 cup (200g) granulated sugar

½ teaspoon salt

1 cup (225g) Roasted Winter Squash Puree (page 238) or canned pumpkin puree

½ teaspoon ground cinnamon

2 tablespoons dark rum

½ cup Salty Caramel Sauce (see variation on page 229)

Whisk the egg yolks together in a glass or stainless steel bowl; set aside.

Combine the cream, milk, sugar, and salt in a saucepan. Cook over medium heat, stirring occasionally, until the mixture begins to bubble around the edges. Ladle about 1 cup of the cream mixture into the egg yolks and whisk vigorously to temper. Pour the egg and cream mixture back into the pot and whisk well to combine.

Cook over medium low heat while stirring constantly with a rubber spatula, being careful not to let the mixture boil, until it thickens enough to coat the back of a spoon, about 7 minutes. Turn off the heat, then whisk in the squash puree, cinnamon, and rum. Strain the mixture through a fine mesh sieve to remove any fibrous bits of squash. Cool completely, at least 4 hours or overnight.

Freeze in an ice cream machine according to the manufacturer's instructions. When it has finished churning, spoon about one third of the ice cream into a freezer-safe container, drizzle half of the caramel sauce on top, and repeat with the remaining ice cream and sauce, finishing with the last third of the ice cream. Cover and freeze until firm, about 4 hours or overnight. Keeps for four days.

WINTER LUXURY PUMPKIN PIE

| MAKES ONE 9-INCH PIE

½ recipe (360g) All-Butter Pie Crust (page 228)

FILLING

2 cups (450g) roasted Winter Luxury pumpkin puree (follow instructions for Roasted Winter Squash Puree, page 238)

¾ cup (180ml) Grade B maple syrup

¾ cup (180ml) heavy cream

½ cup (115g) Crème Fraîche (page 229)

3 eggs, lightly beaten

1 teaspoon vanilla extract (page 235)

¾ teaspoon ground cinnamon

¼ teaspoon ground allspice

⅛ teaspoon freshly grated nutmeg

½ teaspoon salt

TO SERVE

Lightly sweetened whipped cream

A couple of years ago, after visiting an organic farming fair in Maine, I fell in love with the Winter Luxury pumpkin. They are an heirloom variety prized for their caramel flavor and smooth texture and they have beautiful netting on their skin, like a cantaloupe. Substitute roasted butternut squash or canned pumpkin puree if Winter Luxury pumpkins aren't available where you live. If you are concerned about overfilling the pie shell, bake any extra filling alongside the pie in buttered ramekins until it puffs slightly in the center.

To blind-bake the crust: Position a rack in the lower third of the oven and preheat to 400ºF (200ºC). On a lightly floured surface, roll out the pie dough into a roughly 12-inch circle about ⅛ inch thick. Place it in a 9-inch pie pan, fold the edges under, and crimp. Pierce the dough several times with a fork, and chill in the freezer for 15 minutes, or until very firm.

Line the chilled dough with a piece of parchment paper or aluminum foil and fill with pie weights. Bake for 10 minutes, or until the edges are golden. Carefully remove the parchment paper and weights, then bake for 10 to 15 more minutes or until light golden and crisp all over. If the crust puffs up at all while baking gently press it back into the pan with an offset spatula or fork. Turn the oven down to 350ºF (180ºC) and let the crust cool slightly in the oven while you prepare the filling.

To make the filling: Whisk all of the filling ingredients together until well combined. Then use a rubber spatula to press the mixture through a fine-mesh sieve to remove any fibrous bits of squash.

Put the half-baked pie crust on a baking sheet set on the oven rack. Pour the filling into the crust. Slide the rack into the oven and bake until the filling is slightly puffed and the center wiggles just slightly when you gently shake the pan, about 40 to 50 minutes. If the edge of the crust seems like it is burning before the filling is baked, wrap a strip of aluminum foil around the edge to protect it. Cool the pie completely before slicing and serve each piece with a dollop of whipped cream.

winter

On dark, dreary winter days we all need a little something to brighten our spirits. For this important task, I almost always turn to citrus fruit. Whether it's a sweet clementine from the bowl on my table or a lemony chicken soup simmering away on the stove, the lightness of citrus always seems to do the trick. Citrus fruit is unique in that just a bit of its zest can flavor a whole dish, but I like to try to use the whole fruit in my recipes when possible.

Cranberries are the unsung heroes of cold weather baking. Usually relegated to sauce or chutney at Thanksgiving, they can add a pleasant pop of tart flavor and beautiful shot of color to all sorts of desserts, from cakes to crisps to pies, all winter long. Winter is also a great time to utilize dried fruits as the fresh ones become scarce. We always have a container of sticky-sweet medjool dates in my house, and they are the perfect thing to turn into rich desserts that carry us through February and March, when it feels like spring may never come.

CRANBERRIES

CRANBERRIES START TO SHOW UP IN THE MARKET RIGHT AROUND THANKSGIVING, BUT THEY USUALLY STICK AROUND FOR ANOTHER MONTH OR SO. THEIR PLEASANT TARTNESS AND BRIGHT COLOR IS A WONDERFUL ADDITION TO ALL SORTS OF DESSERTS WHEN THE MARKET IS MOSTLY VOID OF COLOR, AND THEY PAIR WELL WITH BOTH APPLES AND PEARS, WHICH ARE AVAILABLE AS STORAGE CROPS IN THE WINTER. LOOK FOR CRANBERRIES WITH FIRM, TAUGHT SKINS; AVOID SOFT BERRIES WITH SURFACE WRINKLES AND BRUISES. CRANBERRIES KEEP EXCEPTIONALLY WELL IN THE REFRIGERATOR OR FREEZER. STORE THEM LOOSELY COVERED IN THE REFRIGERATOR FOR A COUPLE OF WEEKS OR IN A ZIPTOP BAG IN THE FREEZER FOR MONTHS.

CRANBERRY BREAD PUDDING

| MAKES ONE 9 BY 13-INCH PAN

I used to think that bread pudding was a boring, one-note dessert, but in this recipe, pops of tart red cranberries liven up the rich custard-soaked challah. With the addition of a healthy pour of caramel sauce and a dollop of whipped cream, this decadent pudding is special enough to become an addition to your holiday dessert repertoire this year.

1 pound (450g) challah bread, cut into 1-inch (25mm) cubes

2 heaping cups, about 8 ounces (230g) fresh cranberries

½ cup (100g) granulated sugar

1 vanilla bean, or 2 teaspoons vanilla extract

½ teaspoon orange zest

6 large eggs

½ teaspoon salt

3 cups (720ml) whole milk

1 cup (240ml) heavy cream

2 tablespoons dark rum

Crème Fraîche Caramel Sauce or Salty Caramel Sauce variation (page 229), to serve

Unsweetened whipped cream, to serve

Butter a 9 by 13-inch baking dish and fill it with the challah cubes. Sprinkle the cranberries over the top and gently toss the bread and fruit together with your hands to combine.

Use the tip of a knife to slice the vanilla bean in half lengthwise and scrape out the seeds; reserve the pod for another use. In a large bowl, rub the vanilla seeds and orange zest into the sugar with your fingers. Whisk in the eggs and salt, followed by the milk, cream, and rum. Pour the custard through a fine-mesh sieve over the challah in the baking dish. Press gently on the bread cubes so they are more or less covered with the custard. Let sit for 30 minutes to absorb the custard.

While the bread is soaking, position a rack in the center of the oven and preheat to 350ºF (180ºC).

Bake the bread pudding until the custard is set and the bread cubes peeking out of the top start to caramelize, 40 to 50 minutes. Let the bread pudding cool slightly before serving with caramel sauce and whipped cream. This bread pudding is best served warm, the day it's made.

SEASONAL VARIATIONS: In that brief season in the late fall when raspberries and cranberries are both at the market, substitute 1 cup of raspberries for 1 cup of the cranberries. Blueberries, blackberries, and peaches are also wonderful for a summer version.

CORNMEAL AND RICOTTA CAKE WITH CRANBERRIES

| MAKES ONE 8-INCH CAKE

CAKE

1 cup (125g)
all purpose flour

2/3 cup (100g) medium
ground yellow cornmeal

2 teaspoons baking
powder

1/2 teaspoon baking soda

3/4 teaspoon salt

10 tablespoons (140g)
unsalted butter, softened

1 cup (200g)
granulated sugar

2 large eggs, at room
temperature

1 cup (235g) whole
milk ricotta, at room
temperature

1 teaspoon orange zest

1 teaspoon lemon zest

1 slightly heaping cup,
about 4 ounces (115g),
fresh cranberries

GLAZE

3/4 cup (75g) fresh
cranberries

2 cups (240g)
confectioners' sugar

Bright cranberries add a pop of color to this otherwise humble cornmeal cake. Use medium ground cornmeal for this recipe, as coarser ground cornmeal will give the cake a gritty texture. I have included a recipe for a shocking pink and wonderfully tart fresh cranberry glaze below, but the cake is also quite beautiful with a simple dusting of confectioners' sugar instead.

Position a rack in the center of the oven and preheat to 350ºF (180ºC). Butter an 8-inch springform pan or an 8-inch cake pan with sides at least 2 inches tall. Line the pan with parchment paper and butter that, too. Dust the pan and paper with flour.

Whisk the flour, cornmeal, baking powder, baking soda, and salt together. In the bowl of a stand mixer fitted with the paddle attachment cream the butter and sugar together until light and fluffy, about 5 minutes. Add the eggs, one at a time, mixing for 30 seconds after each addition. Add the ricotta and zests and mix for one more minute. Fold in the flour mixture until just combined and then add the cranberries.

Fill the prepared pan with the batter and smooth the top. Bake until a cake tester inserted in the center comes out clean, 40 to 50 minutes. Cool the cake in the pan for 15 minutes, then invert it onto a rack to cool completely.

While the cake is cooling, prepare the glaze: Add the cranberries to the bowl of a food processor fitted with the steel blade and puree. Add the confectioners' sugar and pulse until smooth. The glaze should be thick but pourable. If it seems too thick, add a few drops of water or lemon juice; if it seems too thin, add a bit more confectioners' sugar.

Pour the glaze over the cooled cake and give it about 30 minutes to set before slicing. Store the cake in an airtight container at room temperature for up to three days.

CRANBERRY AND PEAR PANDOWDY

| MAKES ONE 10-INCH PAN

½ recipe (360g) Rye Pie Crust or Spelt Pie Crust (see variations on All-Butter Pie Crust, page 228)

FILLING

½ cup (60g) dried cranberries

4 cups (460g) fresh cranberries

1¼ pounds (565g) ripe but firm pears

½ cup (100g) granulated sugar

1 tablespoon cornstarch

½ teaspoon ground cinnamon

½ cup (120ml) maple syrup

1 teaspoon finely grated fresh ginger

TOPPING

1 egg, lightly beaten for egg wash

1 tablespoon turbinado sugar

TO SERVE

Ice cream or lightly sweetened whipped cream

Pandowdy is a fruit lover's pie because of its low crust-to-fruit ratio. This version calls for dried cranberries for texture, along with tart fresh cranberries and juicy, sweet pears. Take the time to cut the pie crust into circles and shingle them over the fruit to really elevate the appearance of this otherwise humble dessert. Feel free to use any type of pie crust you like for this recipe, but I think the wholesomeness of a rye or spelt crust is quite nice.

Position a rack in the center of the oven and preheat to 375°F (190°C). Lightly butter a 10-inch cast-iron skillet. Line a baking sheet with parchment paper.

Roll the pie crust out onto a lightly floured surface about ⅛ inch thick and use a 2-inch round cookie cutter (or any other shape you like) to cut the crust into circles. Place the circles in a single layer on the baking sheet. Gather the scraps and repeat the process one time, cutting as many circles as possible. Refrigerate the pie crust circles while you prepare the filling.

To make the filling: Put the dried cranberries in a heat-safe bowl and pour boiling water over them to cover. Peel, core, and chop the pears into ¾-inch pieces. Add them to a large bowl and add the fresh cranberries. Drain the dried cranberries, but don't squeeze out the excess liquid. Add those to the bowl, too.

Sprinkle the granulated sugar, cornstarch, and cinnamon over the top. Stir to combine, then add the maple syrup and ginger. Stir again until well combined. Pour the mixture into the prepared skillet and arrange the pie crust circles over the top in a single, slightly overlapping layer. Brush the crust with the egg wash and sprinkle with turbinado sugar.

Set the skillet on a baking sheet and bake until the crust is deep golden brown and the juices are bubbling, 35 to 45 minutes. Let the skillet cool slightly, then spoon the pandowdy into bowls and serve with a scoop of ice cream or a dollop of lightly sweetened whipped cream.

CITRUS

MANY VARIETIES OF CITRUS FRUIT ARE AVAILABLE
YEAR-ROUND, BUT CITRUS TRULY HITS ITS PEAK
IN THE WINTER MONTHS. IT'S DURING THOSE
CHILLY MONTHS THAT WE GET THE BEST VARIETY OF
HONEYED TANGERINES, THIN-SKINNED KUMQUATS,
FLORAL MEYER LEMONS, JUICY BLOOD ORANGES,
AND THE LIKE. WHEN YOU ARE SHOPPING FOR
CITRUS, LOOK FOR FRUITS THAT FEEL HEAVY FOR
THEIR SIZE, WHICH MEANS THEY ARE NICE AND
JUICY, AND TRY TO FIND ORGANIC VARIETIES WHEN
POSSIBLE SO YOU CAN FEEL GOOD ABOUT EATING
EVERY PART OF THE FRUIT, FROM THE OUTSIDE IN.

CHOCOLATE SESAME TART WITH GRAPEFRUIT

| MAKES ONE 13¾ BY 4½-INCH RECTANGULAR TART

*A trio of bitter flavors—chocolate, sesame tahini, and grapefruit—
are combined in this elegant, rich tart. I suggest using semisweet
chocolate here, but if you really love bitter flavors, feel free to use
a chocolate with a higher percentage of cacao. I use chopped chocolate
bars for this recipe rather than chips, as they contain less fillers and
emulsifiers and will make a smoother ganache. Extra grapefruit jam
can be stored in a jar in the fridge for up to two weeks.*

1 recipe Chocolate Tart
Shell (page 234), fully
baked in a rectangular
tart pan

2 medium grapefruit
scrubbed and dried

¾ cup (150g)
granulated sugar

6 ounces (170g) chopped
semisweet (60 percent
cacao or higher) chocolate

½ cup (120ml) heavy
cream

¼ cup (55g) toasted
sesame tahini

1 teaspoon smoked flaky
sea salt, such as Maldon

Grate the zest of one of the grapefruit and measure 1 teaspoon of zest.
Supreme the grapefruit: Cut off the tops and bottoms of the fruits, then
with a very sharp knife, cut the white pith away from the outside of
the fruit. Over a medium saucepan, carefully cut the wedges of fruit
away from the membrane, letting the fruit and juices fall into the pan.
Remove any seeds that have fallen in. Add the sugar and zest to the pan
and stir to combine. Bring the mixture to a boil over high heat and cook,
stirring occasionally, until the grapefruit segments break down and
the mixture thickens and reduces by about half, 7 to 12 minutes. Pour the
mixture into a heat-safe container and let cool to room temperature. It
will seem syrupy right out of the pan, but should be the consistency of
a thick, sticky jam or marmalade when cool.

Add the chopped chocolate to a heat-safe bowl. Bring the cream to a boil in
a saucepan and pour it over the chocolate. Let the mixture sit for 5 minutes,
then whisk until smooth. Whisk in the tahini.

Spread a thin (⅛ to ¼-inch), even layer of the grapefruit marmalade (you
may not use it all) onto the baked and cooled tart shell. Pour the warm
ganache over the top and smooth with an offset spatula. Chill the tart
until firm, at least 1 hour and up to overnight, before serving.

Sprinkle with the smoked salt and cut the tart into thin slices. Store
leftovers in the refrigerator, wrapped in plastic, for up to three days.
The jam will soften the tart shell over time.

BLOOD ORANGE OLD-FASHIONED DONUTS

| MAKES ONE DOZEN DONUTS AND HOLES

DONUTS

2½ cups (285g) cake flour

1½ teaspoons baking powder

¼ teaspoon baking soda

1 teaspoon salt

¼ cup (55g) unsalted butter, softened

½ cup (100g) granulated sugar

1 teaspoon blood orange zest

2 large egg yolks, at room temperature

¾ cup (170g) full-fat yogurt or sour cream, at room temperature

3 tablespoons blood orange juice

1 teaspoon vanilla extract (page 235)

GLAZE

2 blood oranges

3 cups (300g) confectioners' sugar, sifted

Pinch salt

TO FRY

Canola oil

Old-fashioned donuts are humble and unassuming, craggy and cracked. But the addition of a blanket of pink blood orange glaze turns these old-fashioneds into beauty queens. If you've never made fried donuts before, this style is a great place to start because the dough comes together a lot like cookie dough. The dough can also be prepared the day before frying if you want to surprise your friends with donuts for breakfast next time you host brunch at your place.

To make the donuts: Sift the flour, baking powder, baking soda, and salt together into a medium bowl.

In a stand mixer fitted with the paddle attachment, or with a handheld electric mixer, mix the butter, sugar, and orange zest together until sandy. Add the egg yolks and mix for 30 seconds, scraping down the sides of the bowl to ensure even mixing. The mixture should lighten in color and be very thick. Add the yogurt and stir until evenly combined, then add the blood orange juice and vanilla. Add the flour mixture all at once and stir until just combined; use a spatula to scrape down to the bottom of the bowl to ensure even mixing. The dough will be thick and sticky like cookie dough. Wrap the dough in a piece of plastic wrap and refrigerate for at least 1 hour and up to overnight.

Just before frying, make the glaze: Zest of one of the oranges and measure out ½ teaspoon of zest. Juice both of the oranges and measure ¼ cup of juice. Whisk the juice, zest, and salt into the confectioners' sugar until smooth. You want the glaze to be thick but pourable. If the glaze seems thin, add a bit more confectioners' sugar; if it seems too thick, add a bit more orange juice. Set aside while you fry the donuts.

CONTINUED

To fry the donuts: Line a baking sheet with paper towels and set a cooling rack on top. Add enough oil to a Dutch oven or deep-sided skillet to measure a depth of at least 3-inches. Heat the oil over medium high heat until it reaches 350ºF (170ºC) on a candy thermometer.

While the oil is heating, cut the donuts. Lightly flour a baking sheet. Roll the dough out on a well-floured surface to about $\frac{1}{2}$ inch thick. Use a well-floured donut cutter to cut as many donuts and holes as possible; the dough will be soft and sticky, so do your best to handle it gently. Flour the cutter in between each cut to prevent sticking. Gently reroll the scraps and cut again. Transfer the cut donuts and holes to the floured baking sheet. Refrigerate while the oil heats.

When the oil has come up to temperature, dust the excess flour off the donuts and holes and carefully place each one in the hot oil, working in batches and making sure to not crowd the pan; the donuts will expand a bit in the oil. Keep an eye on the temperature of the oil; you may have to raise or lower the heat under the pan to keep the oil at a consistent temperature. Refrigerate the baking sheet with the uncooked donuts in between batches.

Fry each batch of donuts and holes until they are deep golden brown, about 90 seconds, then use a spatula or spider strainer to carefully flip the donuts. Cook the other side for about 90 seconds, or until deep golden brown and cooked through. Remove to the rack until to cool enough to touch, about 5 minutes.

Dip each warm donut in the glaze and let the excess drip off. Return the glazed donuts to the rack, glaze side up, and let them sit until the glaze is no longer sticky. Serve warm or at room temperature. These donuts are best the day they are made.

QUICK MARMALADE WITH BLOOD ORANGES AND MEYER LEMONS

| MAKES ABOUT 4 CUPS (900G)

I love marmalade, but I am kind of a wimp about super bitter flavors, so I tend to go for fine cut marmalades like this one with thin shreds of zest and barely set jelly. Fine marmalades require a bit of careful chopping and preparation of the fruit, but I think the work is worth the time. The small amount of orange-flower water in this recipe barely scents the finished marmalade, but don't skip it, because it elevates it fantastically. I call this "quick" marmalade because it can easily be made in an afternoon, rather than the many-day process of other recipes.

2 pounds (900g) blood oranges (about 8 small oranges)

1 pound (450g) Meyer lemons (about 4 medium lemons)

1 medium lemon

5 cups (1kg) granulated sugar

1 tablespoon orange flower water

2 pint (480ml) or 4 half-pint (240ml) canning jars, sterilized

Bring 2 quarts of water to boil in a large saucepan over high heat. While the water heats, scrub the blood oranges, Meyer lemons, and lemon, removing any excess wax on the fruits' skins. Dry thoroughly. Use a Y-shaped vegetable peeler or sharp paring knife to remove the zest from the fruit in long strips, leaving the white pith behind. Slice the zest strips into fine ribbons, the finer the better. Add the sliced zest to the pot of boiling water and cook until the zest has softened and looks a bit translucent, 25 to 30 minutes.

While the zest cooks, supreme the fruit: Cut off the tops and bottoms off of the fruit and then cut the white pith away from the outside of the fruit. Carefully cut the wedges of fruit away from the membrane, letting the fruit and juices fall into a bowl. Squeeze the remaining membrane to extract all of the juice. Remove any seeds that have fallen into the bowl and tie them tightly in a bit of cheesecloth. The seeds contain pectin, which will help the marmalade set.

Drain the zest strips and reserve the cooking liquid. Rinse the zest strips quickly in cool water.

CONTINUED

QUICK MARMALADE WITH BLOOD ORANGES AND MEYER LEMONS, CONTINUED

Put a couple of teaspoons on a small plate in the freezer. You will use the spoons to test the marmalade for doneness.

To cook the marmalade: In a large nonreactive pot, combine the zest, fruit segments and juice, sugar, ¾ cup of the reserved zest cooking liquid, and the cheesecloth bundle of seeds. Bring the mixture to a rolling boil over high heat. Cook the marmalade, stirring occasionally, until it reaches 220ºF (104ºC), 25 to 35 minutes. Turn off the heat and check the marmalade for doneness by spooning a bit of it into one of the cold spoons. Return the spoon to the plate in the freezer for one minute. After one minute, remove the spoon from the freezer and push the marmalade with your finger. If the surface wrinkles, it's done. If not, cook it for a few more minutes and test again with a clean spoon. Remove the pot from the heat, and use a spoon to press the cheesecloth bundle against the side of the pan to release any juices it has absorbed. Carefully remove the cheesecloth bundle and discard it, then add the orange-flower water.

Ladle the marmalade into clean, sterilized canning jars, leaving ¼ inch of headspace. Let the jars cool to room temperature and store them in the fridge for up to one month.

TANGERINE CREAM PIE

| MAKES ONE 9-INCH PIE

GINGERSNAP CRUST

6 ounces (170g) gingersnap cookies

1 tablespoon granulated sugar

¼ teaspoon ground ginger

Pinch salt

¼ cup (55g) unsalted butter, melted and cooled

TANGERINE FILLING

3 large eggs plus 2 large egg yolks

1 cup (200g) granulated sugar

1 tablespoon cornstarch

¼ teaspoon salt

6 tablespoons freshly squeezed tangerine juice

2 tablespoons freshly squeezed lemon juice

1 tablespoon tangerine zest

1 teaspoon lemon zest

½ teaspoon peeled and finely grated fresh ginger

¼ cup (55g) unsalted butter, cut into ½-inch pieces

INGREDIENTS CONTINUED

Sweet, honeyed tangerines are perfect for eating as a snack just as they are, but when paired with a bit of lemon and ginger they make a very fine, Creamsicle-inspired pie. Here, I have filled a spicy gingersnap crust with tangerine curd spiked with even more ginger, then topped it off with a rich, crème fraîche infused whipped cream.

Position a rack in the center of the oven and preheat to 350ºF (180ºC).

To make the gingersnap crust: Combine the gingersnaps, sugar, ground ginger, and salt in the bowl of a food processor fitted with the steel blade. Process until the cookies are fine crumbs, then remove the lid of the processor and drizzle the melted butter over the top. Put the lid back on and pulse the mixture 8 to 10 times, until all of the crumbs are moistened with butter. Press the crumbs evenly into a 9-inch metal pie pan. Bake the crust until golden brown and fragrant, 10 to 12 minutes. While the crust is cooling, make the filling.

To make the tangerine filling: In a medium saucepan, whisk the eggs, egg yolks, sugar, cornstarch, and salt together. Whisk in the tangerine juice and lemon juice until smooth. Cook the mixture over medium heat, whisking constantly until the mixture has thickened enough to thickly coat the back of a spoon, or has reached 170ºF (76ºC).

Remove the pan from the heat and strain through a fine-mesh sieve to remove any lumps. Shake the strainer to help the curd move through it, but do not press on any solids with a spoon. Whisk in the tangerine zest, lemon zest, and grated ginger, then whisk in the butter piece by piece until well combined.

CONTINUED

TOPPING

1¼ cups (300ml) heavy cream

¼ cup (115g) Crème Fraîche (page 229)

2 tablespoons granulated sugar

½ teaspoon tangerine zest

1 tablespoon finely chopped crystallized ginger

Pour the filling into the prepared crust (it is okay if the crust is still warm from the oven) and return to the oven to bake until set but still slightly wiggly in the center, 10 to 15 minutes. Set the pie on a rack and let it cool to room temperature, then refrigerate until firm, at least 4 hours or overnight before serving.

Just before serving, whip the cream, crème fraîche, and sugar together until soft peaks form. Top the pie with swoops of cream, sprinklings of tangerine zest, and crystallized ginger. This pie is best served the day that it is made.

GRAPEFRUIT AND MEYER LEMON BUNDT CAKE

| MAKES ONE 10-INCH BUNDT CAKE

Most citrusy pound cakes use just the zest and juice to flavor their crumb, but this citrus lover's cake is particularly flavorful because it utilizes grapefruit and Meyer lemon zest, juice, and flesh. The bits of whole fruit are folded into the cake and turn into little jammy pockets that, when baked, are just tart enough balance out the thick coating of sweet, zesty glaze. Don't be tempted to skimp on the glaze; it's the best part.

CAKE

1 medium grapefruit

2 medium Meyer lemons

3 cups (600g) granulated sugar

3 cups (375g) all purpose flour

1/2 teaspoon baking soda

3/4 teaspoon salt

1 cup (225g) unsalted butter, softened

6 large eggs, at room temperature

1 cup (225g) sour cream, at room temperature

GLAZE

2 medium Meyer lemons

3 cups (360g) confectioners' sugar, sifted

Pinch salt

Position a rack in the center of the oven and preheat to 325ºF (160ºC). Butter and flour a 10-inch tube or Bundt pan very thoroughly.

To make the cake: Scrub the grapefruit and lemons with warm soapy water to remove any excess wax, then dry the fruit. Put the sugar into a medium bowl and zest the grapefruit and lemon directly into the sugar. Use your fingers to rub the zest into the sugar until evenly distributed and fragrant.

Supreme the grapefruit and lemons: Cut the tops and bottoms off of all the fruits, then cut the white pith away from the outside of the fruit. Over a bowl, carefully cut the wedges of fruit away from the membrane, letting the fruit and juices fall into the bowl. Remove any seeds that have fallen in and gently break up the fruit into 1/2-inch pieces.

Sift the flour, baking soda, and salt together in a bowl. In the bowl of a stand mixer fitted with the paddle attachment, or in a large bowl with an electric mixer, mix the butter on medium speed for about 2 minutes. Add half of the sugar and zest mixture and turn the mixer up to medium high. Mix for 2 minutes, then add the remaining sugar and mix for 4 minutes, making sure to scrape down the bottom and sides of the bowl with a rubber spatula periodically. The butter and sugar should be very light, fluffy, and fragrant.

CONTINUED

GRAPEFRUIT AND MEYER LEMON BUNDT CAKE, CONTINUED

Add the eggs one at a time, mixing for about 30 seconds after each addition. Periodically stop the mixer and scrape the bottom and sides of the bowl to ensure even mixing.

On low speed, add the sour cream followed by the flour mixture, and mix until just combined. Remove the bowl from the mixer and gently fold in the fruit segments and juices. Pour the batter into the prepared pan and tap the pan lightly on the counter to remove any large air bubbles.

Bake the cake until it is golden and a cake tester inserted in the center comes out clean, 60 to 75 minutes, depending on the pan. Let the cake cool in the pan for 20 minutes, then carefully unmold it onto a rack to cool a bit more before glazing.

To make the glaze: Zest and juice the lemons. Add the zest, confectioners' sugar, and a pinch of salt to a bowl. Whisk in about 6 tablespoons of the lemon juice. You want the glaze to be thick, but pourable. If the glaze seems too thick to pour, add a few more drops of lemon juice.

When the cake has mostly cooled, use a skewer to poke a few holes into its surface. Drizzle half of the glaze on top of the cake, let it soak in for about 20 minutes, then whisk the remaning glaze until smooth and pour it over the top of the cake. Let the glaze set for a few minutes before serving.

Store leftover cake in an airtight container at room temperature for up to three days.

PRESERVED LEMON ICE CREAM

| MAKES ABOUT 1 QUART (900G)

I like to make a big batch of lemons preserved in salt each winter to last me through the year. They are most commonly used in savory cooking, but in this ice cream they add lovely sour and salty notes to rich lemon ice cream. Serve scoops of this sweet and salty treat in elegant little dishes with small pour of fruity olive oil and a sprinkle of sea salt on top for an unexpectedly complex treat.

4 large egg yolks

1 cup (240ml) whole milk

2 cups (480ml) heavy cream

1 cup (200g) granulated sugar

¼ cup (60ml) freshly squeezed lemon juice

3 tablespoons finely chopped Preserved Lemon rind (page 237)

½ teaspoon salt, or to taste

¼ cup (60ml) fruity olive oil, plus more to serve

Flaky sea salt, to serve (optional)

Whisk the egg yolks together in a glass or stainless steel bowl; set aside. Combine the milk, cream, and sugar in a saucepan. Cook over medium heat, stirring occasionally, until the mixture begins to bubble around the edges. Ladle about 1 cup of the cream mixture into the egg yolks and whisk vigorously to temper. Pour the egg and cream mixture back into the pan and whisk well to combine.

Cook the mixture on medium low heat while stirring constantly and being careful not to let the mixture boil, until it thickens enough to coat the back of a spoon, about 7 minutes. Whisk in the lemon juice and preserved lemon rind. Add the salt to taste. Cool the mixture completely, for at least 4 hours or overnight.

Just before churning, whisk in the olive oil, then freeze in an ice cream machine according to manufacturer's instructions. Transfer the ice cream to a freezer-safe container, cover, and freeze until firm, about 4 hours or overnight. Serve scoops of ice cream in dishes with a drizzle of fruity olive oil and a sprinkle of salt. Keeps in the freezer for four days.

RANGPUR LIME BARS WITH SAFFRON

| MAKES SIXTEEN 2-INCH BARS

CRUST

1 cup (125g)
all purpose flour

3 tablespoons granulated sugar

1 tablespoon cornstarch

¼ teaspoon salt

½ cup (115g) unsalted butter, softened

FILLING

¼ teaspoon saffron threads

¾ cup (150g) granulated sugar

2 teaspoons Rangpur lime zest

1 tablespoon cornstarch

¼ teaspoon salt

4 large eggs

½ cup (120ml) Rangpur lime juice

3 tablespoons unsalted butter, melted and cooled slightly

TO SERVE

2 tablespoons confectioners' sugar

I had my first Rangpur lime about three years ago, and I fell in love with its spicy and tart flavor. Every year in January and February, I seek them out at my local specialty stores, and sometimes my very generous friend in California who grows them in her yard ships me a box. They are very juicy, so you'll only need a couple to make up the half cup (120ml) of juice called for here. Rangpur limes can be hard to find, so use Persian limes or key limes if they are not available.

Position a rack in the center of the oven and preheat to 350ºF (180ºC). Line an 8-inch square baking pan with foil and butter the foil.

To make the crust: Whisk the flour, sugar, cornstarch, and salt together. Add the butter and mix with a wooden spoon or rubber spatula until well combined. Press the dough evenly into the bottom of the pan. Bake until golden brown, about 20 minutes.

While the crust is baking, prepare the filling. Use a mortar and pestle to grind the saffron threads with a pinch of the sugar to a fine powder, then stir in 1 tablespoon of boiling water to bloom.

Add the rest of the sugar and the lime zest to a medium bowl. Rub the zest into the sugar until well combined and fragrant. Stir in the cornstarch and salt. Whisk in the eggs, followed by the lime juice, the saffron threads and their liquid, and the butter until well combined.

When the crust is finished baking, turn the oven down to 300ºF (150ºC). Pour the filling over the hot crust and return the pan to the oven. Bake until the filling is set but still slightly wiggly in the center, about 20 more minutes. Cool the bars completely in the pan, then lift the bars out of the pan, using the foil as handles. Cut into any shape you like and dust with confectioners' sugar just before serving. Store the bars in the refrigerator in an airtight container for up to three days.

GINGERY LIME POSSET

| MAKES SIX 6-OUNCE CUSTARDS

Posset is about as old school as dessert gets—we're talking medieval here—but the method definitely holds up over time. These little custards are super simple to make, and just as delicious as some more labor intensive custards and puddings. They can also be made with lemon or grapefruit juice, but I think the floral sweetness of the lime is particularly nice here with a bit of fresh ginger. Garnish each custard with a sprinkling of chopped crystallized ginger, lime zest, and a dollop of cream, if you like.

2 cups (480ml) heavy cream

½ cup (100g) granulated sugar

6 tablespoons (90ml) lime juice

1 teaspoon lime zest

½ teaspoon peeled and finely grated fresh ginger

Pinch salt

Chopped crystallized ginger, to serve (optional)

Lime zest, to serve

Lightly sweetened whipped cream, to serve (optional)

Combine the cream and sugar in a large saucepan—use a bigger pan than you think you might need, as the cream will foam quite a bit—at least 3 quarts. Bring the mixture to a boil, stirring occasionally, and let it boil, for 3 minutes. Remove from the heat and let cool for 5 minutes. Whisk in the lime juice, lime zest, ginger, and salt. Divide the mixture among six 6-ounce ramekins and refrigerate until set and firm, about 4 hours or overnight.

Serve the possets with a sprinkle of crystallized ginger, lime zest, and a dollop of cream each, if desired.

If you are going to let these sit in the fridge overnight, cover each ramekin with plastic wrap.

CITRUS ALMOND THUMBPRINTS WITH SUMMER JAM

| MAKES 15 TO 18 COOKIES

1¾ cups (220g) all purpose flour

¾ cup (85g) almond flour

½ teaspoon salt, plus a pinch

1 cup (225g) unsalted butter, softened but cool

½ cup (100g) sugar, plus 2 teaspoons

3 large egg yolks

1 teaspoon lemon zest

½ teaspoon orange zest

1 teaspoon vanilla extract (page 235)

¼ teaspoon almond extract

1 egg white

⅓ cup (75g) homemade or high-quality store-bought jam

At the restaurant where I used to work, we made a lot of tiny cookies for our tea service. I probably made tens of thousands of cookies by the end of my five-year stretch in that kitchen, but my favorites were the jam-filled thumbprints. I always liked the ones filled with raspberry and apricot jam, but use any jam you like.

Position a rack in the center of the oven and preheat to 350ºF (180ºC). Line two baking sheets with parchment paper.

Stir the flours and salt together in a small bowl. In another bowl, cream the butter and ½ cup sugar together with an electric mixer on medium high until light and fluffy. Add the egg yolks all at once and mix until well combined. Mix in the zests and extracts, then add the flour mixture all at once and stir until just combined. Make sure to scrape down to the bottom of the bowl to ensure that the flour mixture is well distributed.

Scoop cookies onto the prepared baking sheets in roughly 1-inch balls, about 2 inches apart. Use your finger or the handle of a wooden spoon to make an indent in the center of each cookie. In a small bowl, whisk the egg white with the pinch of salt. Brush the surface of each cookie with this egg wash, and sprinkle with the 2 teaspoons of sugar. Fill each indent with about ½ teaspoon of jam, being careful not to overfill. Chill the cookies in the refrigerator for 30 minutes before baking.

Bake the cookies until shiny and barely golden, 10 to 12 minutes. Let them cool completely on the baking sheets, then store in an airtight container at room temperature for up to three days.

VARIATION: These thumbprint cookies call for almond flour, but the almond can easily be replaced with just about any other finely ground nut flour; ground hazelnuts are wonderful with strawberry jam, and walnuts are tasty with apricot jam (page 67).

DATES

DATES HAVE BEEN A PART OF MANY CUISINES
FOR CENTURIES, BUT IN RECENT YEARS THEY HAVE
BECOME VERY POPULAR AND ARE EASY TO FIND
IN MOST MARKETS. I ESPECIALLY LIKE TO USE
DATES IN THE WINTER WHEN SWEET, FRESH FRUIT
IS SCARCE. I PREFER MEDJOOL DATES, SOMETIMES
CALLED THE "KING OF DATES," FOR BAKING
BECAUSE OF THEIR LARGE SIZE AND SOFT FLESH.
FRESH DATES SHOULD BE SOFT AND STICKY AND
HAVE A CARAMELIZED SWEET FLAVOR. HARD, DRY
DATES WITH FLAKY SKIN ARE A BIT PAST THEIR
PRIME AND SHOULD BE AVOIDED. DATES CAN BE
TOUGH TO CHOP WITH A KNIFE BECAUSE THEY
ARE SO STICKY, SO I OFTEN PIT THEM WITH MY
FINGERS, THEN USE A PAIR OF KITCHEN SHEARS
TO SNIP THEM IN SMALLER PIECES.

STICKY TOFFEE PUDDING WITH CRANBERRIES

| MAKES ONE 9-INCH SQUARE CAKE

CAKE

2 cups (300g) Medjool dates

1¼ cups (300ml) boiling water

½ teaspoon baking soda

1½ cups (190g) all purpose flour

1 teaspoon baking powder

½ teaspoon salt

¼ teaspoon ground cinnamon

⅛ teaspoon ground cloves

6 tablespoons (70g) unsalted butter, softened

¾ cup (150g) firmly packed dark brown sugar

2 large eggs, at room temperature

1 tablespoon brandy

½ teaspoon orange zest

1¼ cups (140g) cranberries

BRANDIED TOFFEE SAUCE

½ cup (115g) butter

⅔ cup (135g) firmly packed dark brown sugar

⅔ cup (180ml) heavy cream

2 tablespoons brandy

Pinch salt

Whipped cream

Sticky toffee pudding is an ideal winter dessert: rich, warm, and comforting. It is traditionally served with toffee sauce, and this version is no different, though I have added brandy to the sauce for a little punch. If you don't have fresh cranberries use frozen.

Position a rack in the center of the oven and preheat it to 350ºF (180ºC). Butter and flour a 9-inch square baking pan.

To make the cake: Pit and chop the dates and put them in a heat-safe bowl with the baking soda. Pour the boiling water over the top and stir to combine. Let the dates soak while you prepare the rest of the cake.

Whisk the flour, baking powder, salt, and spices together in a small bowl. In the bowl of a stand mixer fitted with the paddle attachment, or in a large bowl with a handheld electric mixer, cream the butter and sugar together until light and fluffy. Add in the eggs one at a time, mixing for 30 seconds after each addition, then add the brandy and orange zest. Add in the date mixture and stir to combine. Switch to a rubber spatula and scrape the bottom and sides of the bowl to ensure that the batter is evenly mixed. Fold in the flour mixture until just combined, then fold in the cranberries.

Pour the batter into the prepared pan and tap gently on the countertop to release any air bubbles. Bake the cake until it is puffed, golden, and a cake tester inserted into the center comes out clean, 25 to 30 minutes.

To make the sauce: Combine the butter, sugar, and cream in a medium saucepan over medium heat. Bring the mixture to a simmer, whisking often, and cook until smooth and thickened, about 7 minutes. Whisk in the brandy and salt.

Serve warm, topped with a generous pour of warm toffee sauce and a dollop of unsweetened whipped cream. This cake is best served the day that it's made, but keeps for a day or two in the fridge. Rewarm slightly in a 350ºF (180ºC) oven before serving.

BROWNED-BUTTER DATE BLONDIES

| MAKES 16 TO 24 BLONDIES

These blondies are admittedly a bit over the top: packed with browned butter, toasted nuts, dried fruit, and chocolate, but what is winter without a little indulgence? Given their richness, serve them in small squares. The baked blondies keep for a couple of weeks in the freezer in an airtight container or ziptop bag.

1 cup (100g) coarsely chopped walnuts

1 cup (225g) unsalted butter

2 cups (400g) firmly packed light brown sugar

3 large eggs, at room temperature

2 tablespoons bourbon, optional

1 tablespoon vanilla extract (page 235)

2 teaspoons salt

2 cups (250g) all purpose flour

¾ teaspoon baking powder

1 cup (150g) Medjool dates, pitted and chopped

1 cup (170g) chopped bittersweet chocolate or chocolate chips

¼ cup (30g) dried cherries, roughly chopped

Position a rack in the center of the oven and preheat to 350°F (180°C). Line a 9 by 9-inch baking pan (for thick blondies) or 9 by 13-inch pan (for thin blondies) with foil or parchment paper, and grease well.

Arrange the walnuts in a single layer on a baking sheet. Slide into the oven and toast until golden. Slice the butter into tablespoon-size pieces, put it in a light-colored saucepan over medium heat, and melt it, stirring constantly. The melted butter will foam a bit, but then the foam will subside. Keep cooking the butter, stirring occasionally, until the milk solids turn golden brown and the butter has a nutty fragrance, 7 to 10 minutes. Take the butter off the heat and pour it, along with all of the browned bits, from the pan into a heat-safe bowl to cool slightly.

In a large bowl, whisk the sugar, eggs, bourbon, vanilla, and salt together. Whisk in the cooled butter, then fold in the flour and baking powder.

Make sure that the mixture is almost at room temperature (to prevent the chocolate from melting), then stir in the toasted walnuts, dates, chocolate, and cherries. Spoon the batter into the prepared pan and smooth the top.

Bake until the top is shiny, set, and slightly cracked around the edges, 25 to 35 minutes for thin blondies and 35 to 45 minutes for thick blondies. Transfer the pan to a wire rack and let cool completely. When cool, lift the blondies out of the pan using the parchment paper or foil as handles and slice into 16 to 24 squares.

YEAR-ROUND ESSENTIALS

In this chapter, you'll find a collection of recipes that I think are worth mastering. They are the pie crusts, pastry doughs, and pantry staples I turn to again and again throughout the year to highlight all sorts of fruit.

You may have noticed that I like using whole grain flours in my baking; it's mostly because I think they are delicious. Whole grain flours add a depth of flavor and texture that pairs so nicely with fruit in desserts. They also generally contain more oils than all purpose flour, which means that they can go rancid quite quickly. To offset this, buy flours in smaller quantities if you don't think you'll use them all that often, and store extra flour in airtight containers in the freezer for long-term freshness.

A bit about the flours I like to use:

ALL PURPOSE As the name suggests, all purpose is the flour most used in this book. I prefer unbleached all purpose flour for baking. Brands vary based on where you live, but look for flour that is milled close to where you live, this will ensure that the flour is as fresh as possible.

BUCKWHEAT Buckwheat flour has an assertive, bitter flavor that can be overwhelming to some, but when blended with other flavors, that bitter quality can make a fine counterpoint. Because buckwheat flour does not contain gluten, it isn't the best for flaky pie crust or breads that require gluten for stability, but it is a perfect addition to a crisp Buckwheat Tart Shell (page 233) and Cacao Nib Poppy Seed Wafers (page 39).

RYE Rye flour comes in light and dark varieties. For the recipes in this book, I used finely milled whole grain dark rye flour. Rye flour has a slightly milky and tangy flavor that pairs wonderfully with berries and stone fruit. It is especially nice to blend rye and all purpose flours to make an all-butter pie crust.

SPELT Spelt flour is similar to whole wheat flour, but it is a bit lighter in both flavor and texture. Its low gluten content ensures that it bakes super tender and crisp. I love to combine it with all purpose flour to make Spelt Quick Puff Pastry (page 231), which I keep in my freezer at all times.

WHOLE WHEAT Whole wheat flour is probably the most available and most used whole grain flour. It has a wonderfully earthy flavor, texture, and scent. Brands of whole wheat flour can vary quite a bit in taste and texture so I like to look for flour that is finely milled. It can also make baked goods quite heavy, so I like to blend it with other flours, usually all purpose, to ensure that the finished baked goods have nice texture.

ALL-BUTTER PIE CRUST

MAKES ABOUT 25 OUNCES (720G), ENOUGH FOR ONE
DOUBLE CRUST OR TWO SINGLE CRUST PIES

*All pie crust is made from the same basic
ingredients: flour, fat, water, and salt. I am
partial to an all-butter crust because I think
it tastes the best. The key to flaky pie crust
is to keep the ingredients nice and cold—
especially the butter and water—and to
work quickly and intentionally. The small
amount of apple cider vinegar in this recipe
helps tenderize the dough by preventing
the gluten in the flour from forming long
strands, making the dough tough. I like to
mix pie crust with my hands rather than a
food processor or pastry blender because I can
control the exact size and shape of the butter
pieces for the flakiest results.*

2 2/3 cups (340g) all purpose flour

1 teaspoon salt

1 cup plus 2 tablespoons (255g) very
cold unsalted butter

1 tablespoon apple cider vinegar

8 tablespoons (120ml) ice water

Whisk the flour and salt together in a large
bowl, cut the butter into 1/2-inch cubes, and add
the apple cider vinegar to the ice water.

Working quickly, add the butter to the flour and
toss to coat. Then use your fingers or the palms
of your hands to press each cube of butter into a
flat sheet. Keep tossing the butter in the flour as
you go to ensure that each butter piece is coated

with flour. The idea is to create flat, thin shards
of butter that range from about the size of a
dime to about the size of a quarter.

If at any time the butter seems warm or soft,
briefly refrigerate the bowl.

Sprinkle about 6 tablespoons of the icy cold
vinegar-water mixture over the flour mixture.
Use a gentle hand or wooden spoon to stir the
water into the flour until just combined. If the
dough seems dry, add more cold water a couple
of teaspoons at a time. You have added enough
water when you can pick up a handful of the
dough and easily squeeze it together without it
falling apart.

Press the dough together, then split it in half.
Form each half into a disk, and wrap each disk in
plastic wrap. Chill the dough for at least 2 hours
before using, but preferably overnight. Keeps for
up to three months in the freezer wrapped in a
double layer of plastic wrap and a layer of foil.
Thaw in the refrigerator before using.

VARIATIONS: For a rye variation, substitute
1 1/3 cups (175g) rye flour for an equal amount
of the all purpose flour. For a spelt variation,
substitute 1 1/3 cups (175g) spelt flour for an equal
amount of the all purpose flour. You also may
need a bit more water to bind the dough for
these variations.

CRÈME FRAÎCHE

MAKES ABOUT 1 CUP (225G)

Crème fraîche is a tart French-style sour cream. It is a bit more subtle in flavor than American sour cream, and I love to use it both as a garnish and as an ingredient in sweet and savory cooking. It can sometimes be difficult to find at the grocery store, but it is very simple to make at home. Add a tablespoon or two of maple syrup to the finished crème fraîche for a slightly sweet variation.

1 cup (240ml) heavy cream

2 tablespoons buttermilk

Stir the cream and buttermilk together in a glass container. Cover and let sit at room temperature for 12 to 24 hours, or until the cream has thickened to the consistency of soft sour cream and has a tart, tangy flavor. Store the crème fraîche in the refrigerator, covered, for up to seven days.

CRÈME FRAÎCHE CARAMEL SAUCE

MAKES ABOUT 1½ CUPS (360ML)

This sauce is the kind of thing that someone might say makes shoe leather palatable. I love to drizzle it on pies (Pear Pie with Crème Fraîche Caramel, page 161), tarts, bread pudding (Cranberry Bread Pudding, page 186) or ice cream. Heck, sometimes I just eat it out of the jar with a spoon.

1 cup (200g) granulated sugar

¼ cup (60ml) water

1 teaspoon sea salt

½ cup (115g) unsalted butter, cut into tablespoon-size pieces

1 vanilla bean, split lengthwise and seeds scraped from the pod

½ cup (115g) Crème Fraîche (page 229), at room temperature

Combine the sugar, water, and salt in a medium saucepan. Cook the mixture over medium high heat, swirling the pan occasionally until the sugar dissolves, but do not stir. Add the butter, and vanilla seeds and pod. Cook, swirling the pan occasionally so that the mixture browns evenly, but do not stir, until it is amber in color. Don't walk away from the pot during this process, as the caramel will go from perfectly amber to burned in mere moments.

Once the caramel is deep amber in color, remove the pan from the heat and carefully whisk in the crème fraîche until the sauce is smooth. The caramel may bubble violently, so watch for splatters. Carefully remove the vanilla pod, rinse it off, and reserve it for another use. Cool the sauce slightly before using. Store the sauce in the refrigerator an airtight jar with a lid for up to one week. Warm slightly before serving.

VARIATION: You can easily make this into Salty Caramel Sauce by increasing the sea salt to 2 teaspoons and swapping out the crème fraîche for an equal amount of heavy cream.

CRISP TOPPING

MAKES ABOUT 3½ CUPS (390G), ENOUGH FOR ONE LARGE CRISP OR TWO PIES

Fruit crisp is a great back-pocket dessert that you can make any time of year at the drop of a hat.

1 cup (125g) all purpose flour

½ cup (45g) old-fashioned oats

½ cup (100g) firmly packed light brown sugar

½ teaspoon salt

¼ teaspoon baking powder

½ cup (115g) unsalted butter, softened but cool

Combine all of the ingredients except for the butter in a medium bowl and give a quick stir to combine, making sure to break up any lumps of brown sugar. Add the butter and use your fingertips to mix everything together until crumbs form. Use the mixture immediately, or store in a ziptop bag in the freezer for up to one month. You can use the crisp topping straight from the freezer; just add a couple of extra minutes to the baking time of your crisp or pie.

VARIATIONS: Substitute ½ cup (65g) of rye flour or ½ cup (65g) of whole wheat flour for an equal amount of the all purpose flour; add ½ cup (about 60g) of chopped nuts (walnuts, pecans, almonds, or hazelnuts); or spice things up with up to ¾ teaspoon of ground cinnamon and/or ground cardamom.

PASTRY CREAM

MAKES ABOUT 2 CUPS (450G)

Pastry cream is a rich, thick custard that can be used to fill cream puffs, tarts, or éclairs, or in between cake layers. This version is flavored with vanilla bean, which I find to be the most versatile, but you can also add a splash of almond extract, up to 1 teaspoon of citrus zest, or whisk in a handful of finely chopped chocolate, to flavor the finished pastry cream. I often lighten pastry cream with whipped cream or mascarpone when I use it to fill tarts.

2 cups (480ml) whole milk

1 vanilla bean, split in half lengthwise to expose the seeds

4 large egg yolks

⅔ cup (130g) granulated sugar

3 tablespoons (25g) cornstarch

¼ teaspoon salt

Heat the milk and vanilla bean in a medium saucepan over medium heat until just simmering. Turn off the heat and let the milk steep for 1 hour. Remove the vanilla bean and scrape all of the delicious seeds into the milk. Rinse the pod and save it for another use. Reheat the milk over medium heat until it is bubbling around the edges.

While the milk is reheating, in a large bowl, whisk the egg yolks, sugar, cornstarch, and salt until very light yellow in color. The mixture will be thick and lumpy at first, but will smooth out after a few strokes. Slowly stream in about half of the hot milk while whisking constantly, then transfer the mixture back to the pot with the remaining milk. Cook the mixture over medium low heat, whisking constantly, until it begins to bubble big, lazy bubbles. Once the mixture begins to bubble, whisk it vigorously for 1 minute to cook the cornstarch completely. Remove from the heat and pour the mixture through a fine-mesh sieve to remove any lumps. Store the cream in the refrigerator with a layer of plastic wrap pressed on the surface to prevent a skin from forming. Keeps in the refrigerator for up to two days.

SPELT QUICK PUFF PASTRY

MAKES ABOUT 3 POUNDS (1350G) PASTRY, ENOUGH FOR THREE LARGE TARTS OR LOTS AND LOTS OF LITTLE ONES

The method to make this quick puff pastry is a lot less involved than traditional puff pastry, but the results are still spectacularly flaky. The addition of spelt flour gives the pastry a bit of nutty flavor and a delicate, crisp texture when baked. Because this dough is unsweetened, you can use it for both sweet and savory preparations. This dough can used for Cherry and Chocolate Turnovers (page 50) and Marie-Danielle's Apple Tart (page 146).

3 cups (680g) cold unsalted butter

2¼ cups (280g) all purpose flour

2¼ cups (290g) spelt flour

2 teaspoons salt

1 cup (240ml) cold water

Cut the cold butter into ½-inch cubes. In the bowl of a stand mixer fitted with the paddle attachment or in a large bowl, combine the flours and salt. Add the butter all at once and mix on low speed until the butter is well coated with flour and beginning to break up into smaller pieces. If working by hand, use a pastry blender for this step. Add the water all at once and mix for about 15 seconds, or until the water is evenly incorporated. At this point the dough may look like a crumbly mess: don't worry about it.

Turn the mixture out onto a clean, lightly floured work surface and do your best to pat it into a rectangle about 1 inch thick with your hands. Use a bench scraper to fold the right third of the dough to the center. Fold the left third of the dough over the other two thirds, like a letter. Turn the dough 90 degrees. You have completed your first turn. If the dough is sticking to the work surface, lightly flour it, but take care not to add too much more flour to the dough.

Press the dough back into a rectangle roughly 1 inch thick and repeat the process two more times. The dough will seem crumbly, and may fall apart a bit at first, but it will come together eventually. If at any point the bits of butter seem soft, slide the dough onto a baking sheet and refrigerate for a few minutes, until the butter has hardened up a bit. By the end of the first three turns, the dough will begin to resemble a cohesive mass.

CONTINUED

After three turns, wrap the dough in plastic wrap and move it into the fridge for 1 hour to chill and rest. You can leave the dough in the fridge overnight, well wrapped, at this stage if you like. Just make sure to give it a little time to warm up before moving on to the next step.

After the dough has rested, use a rolling pin to complete the last three turns. On a lightly floured surface, roll the dough into a rectangle just under ½ inch thick and repeat the letter folds just as before. Repeat two more times. Wrap the dough in plastic wrap and let it rest in the refrigerator for at least one hour before using. If you don't plan to use the dough immediately, divide it into three pieces, each weighing about 1 pound, and wrap each in a double layer of plastic wrap. This dough will keep up to two days in the refrigerator or, wrapped in an additional layer of foil, in the freezer for up to three months. Thaw frozen dough in the refrigerator before using.

SWEET TART SHELL THREE WAYS: ALL-PURPOSE, BUCKWHEAT, CHOCOLATE

Like pie crust, tart shells are a versatile way to showcase seasonal fruit. They can be filled with everything from fresh fruit to jam to pastry cream or whipped cream. Below are my three favorite versions. The all-purpose tart shell is crisp, buttery, and just lightly sweet. The slightly bitter and nutty flavor of buckwheat is wonderful with ultrasweet summer berries and stone fruits. The chocolate

tart shell pairs nicely with citrus flavors in the winter, but is also wonderful filled with vanilla pastry cream and topped with berries in the spring and summer.

These crisp and buttery tart shells can be pressed into the pan immediately after mixing or wrapped in plastic, chilled, and rolled out. I have a strong preference for the latter method because I feel it results in a more even thickness, but both work just fine. For both methods, make sure to chill the shell very thoroughly before baking to reduce shrinkage.

ALL-PURPOSE TART SHELL

MAKES ONE 10-INCH (25CM) ROUND, ONE 13¾ BY 4½-INCH (35 BY 11CM) RECTANGLE, OR SIX 4-INCH (10CM) TART SHELLS

1½ cups (195g) all purpose flour

⅓ cup (40g) confectioners' sugar

½ teaspoon salt

9 tablespoons (125g) cold unsalted butter, cut into ¼-inch cubes

1 large egg yolk

1 teaspoon vanilla extract (page 235)

2 tablespoons cold water, as needed

In the bowl of a food processor fitted with the steel blade or in a bowl using a pastry blender, combine the flour, confectioners' sugar, and salt. Pulse to combine. Add the butter and pulse until it is the size of small peas. Add the egg yolk and vanilla and pulse until evenly distributed. Pulse in the cold water until the dough starts to hold together. It will appear to be a bit crumbly, but should hold together easily when pressed.

Lightly butter a tart pan and press the dough into the pan. Make sure to evenly coat the bottom and sides with $\frac{1}{8}$- to $\frac{1}{4}$-inch of dough. Save a bit of dough just in case you have to repair any cracks after baking the shell. Alternately press the dough into a disk, wrap the disk in plastic wrap and refrigerate for 30 minutes, then roll the dough out on a lightly floured surface to a $\frac{1}{8}$- to $\frac{1}{4}$-inch thickness and transfer it to the pan. Press the dough into the corners and up the sides of the pan. Trim the edges so they are even with the top of the tart pan. Save the trimmings in case you have to repair any cracks after baking the shell. Prick the bottom and sides of the tart shell several times with a fork, then freeze it for 30 minutes.

Preheat the oven to 375ºF (190ºC) and line the tart shell with a piece of aluminum foil, shiny side down. Bake the tart shell until it is beginning to brown, about 15 minutes, then remove the foil and continue to bake until the shell is golden brown all over, 10 to 15 more minutes. If the shell puffs up while baking, carefully use an offset spatula to gently press it back into the pan. Repair any cracks that may have formed with the reserved dough. Baked shells or unbaked dough will keep in the freezer, well wrapped, for up to three months. Thaw in the refrigerator before filling baked shells or using unbaked dough.

BUCKWHEAT TART SHELL

MAKES ONE 10-INCH (25CM) ROUND, ONE 13¾ BY 4½-INCH (35 BY 11CM) RECTANGLE, OR SIX 4-INCH (10CM) TART SHELLS

1 cup (140g) buckwheat flour

½ cup (63g) all purpose flour

½ cup (60g) confectioners' sugar

½ teaspoon salt

1 large egg yolk

9 tablespoons (125g) cold unsalted butter, cut into ¼-inch cubes

1 tablespoon cold water, as needed

In the bowl of a food processor fitted with the steel blade or in a large bowl using a pastry blender, combine the flours, sugar, and salt. Pulse to combine. Add the butter and pulse until it is the size of small peas. Add the egg yolk and pulse until it is evenly distributed. Pulse in the cold water until the dough starts to hold together. It will appear to be a bit crumbly, but should hold together easily when pressed. If the dough doesn't seem to be holding together, add a bit more ice water 1 teaspoon at a time. Turn the dough out onto a clean surface and knead it a couple of times to form a ball.

Lightly butter a tart pan and press the dough into the pan, making sure to evenly coat the bottom and sides with $\frac{1}{8}$- to $\frac{1}{4}$-inch of dough. Save a bit of extra dough in case you have to repair any cracks later on. Or wrap the dough in plastic wrap and refrigerate for 30 minutes, then roll it out on a lightly floured surface to a $\frac{1}{8}$- to $\frac{1}{4}$-inch thickness and transfer it to the pan. Trim the

CONTINUED

edges so they are even with the top of the tart pan. Save the trimmings in case you have to repair any cracks after baking the shell. Prick the bottom and sides of the tart shell several times with a fork, then freeze for 30 minutes.

Preheat the oven to 375ºF (190ºC) and line the frozen shell with a piece of aluminum foil, shiny side down. Bake the tart shell until it is beginning to brown, about 15 minutes, then remove the foil and continue to bake until the shell is golden brown all over, 10 to 15 more minutes. If the shell puffs up while baking, carefully use an offset spatula to gently press it back into the pan. Repair any cracks that may have formed with the reserved dough. Baked shells or unbaked dough will keep in the freezer, well wrapped, for up to three months. Thaw in the refrigerator before filling baked shells or using unbaked dough.

CHOCOLATE TART SHELL

MAKES ONE 10-INCH (25CM) ROUND, ONE 13¾ BY 4½-INCH (35 BY 11CM) RECTANGLE, OR EIGHT 4-INCH (10CM) TART SHELLS

1 large egg plus 1 large egg yolk

1 teaspoon vanilla extract (page 235)

1½ cups (195g) all purpose flour

⅓ cup (33g) cocoa powder

⅓ cup (67g) firmly packed light brown sugar

½ teaspoon instant espresso powder

½ teaspoon salt

10 tablespoons (140g) cold unsalted butter, cut into ¼-inch cubes

1 tablespoon cold water, as needed

Whisk the whole egg, egg yolk, and vanilla together in a small bowl. In the bowl of a food processor fitted with the steel blade or in a bowl using a pastry blender, combine the flour, cocoa powder, sugar, espresso powder, and salt. Pulse to combine. Add the butter and pulse until it is the size of small peas. Add the egg mixture and pulse until it is evenly distributed and the dough starts to hold together. It may appear to be a bit crumbly, but should hold together easily when pressed. If the dough does not hold together when pressed, pulse in the water 1 teaspoon at a time.

Lightly butter a tart pan and press the dough into the pan, making sure to evenly coat the bottom and sides with ⅛- to ¼-inch of dough. Save a bit of dough just in case you have to repair any cracks after baking the shell. Or press the dough into a disk, wrap the disk in plastic wrap, and refrigerate for 30 minutes. Roll the dough out on a lightly floured surface to a ⅛-to ¼-inch thickness and transfer it to the pan. Press the dough into the corners and up the sides of the pan. Trim the edges so they are even with the top of the tart pan. Save the trimmings in case you have to repair any cracks after baking the shell. Freeze the shell for 30 minutes.

Preheat the oven to 375ºF (190ºC) and line the frozen shell with a piece of aluminum foil, shiny side down. Bake the tart shell (no need for pie weights) until it is beginning to brown, about 15 minutes, then remove the foil and continue to bake until the shell is completely cooked through. If the shell puffs up while baking, carefully use an offset spatula to gently press it back into the pan. Repair any cracks that may have formed with the reserved dough. Baked shells or unbaked dough will keep in the freezer, well wrapped, for up to three months. Thaw in the refrigerator before filling baked shells or using unbaked dough.

VANILLA EXTRACT

MAKES 1 CUP (240ML)

You may have noticed that I use vanilla beans a lot in this book, which I know can be prohibitively expensive. But vanilla beans are quite economical if you buy them in bulk online. I tend to buy a pound of beans once a year, which is enough to make a big batch of vanilla extract, use whole in recipes, and even give some away to friends. If you don't think you can use an entire pound of beans (usually about fifty), it is worth it to ask a friend or two to split an order with you. Feel free to use this ratio to make more or less extract, depending on your needs.

6 vanilla beans

1 cup (240ml) vodka

1 glass jar or bottle with a tight fitting lid

Slice each vanilla bean in half lengthwise and place them in a glass jar or bottle. Trim the beans to fit the jar if necessary. Pour the vodka over the top, and make sure the beans are completely covered with alcohol. Screw the lid on tightly and give the jar a good shake. Put the jar in a dark, cool place (but not somewhere you'll forget about it) and let it infuse for at least two months before using. Shake the jar every couple of days. After two months, you can strain the extract into another bottle to remove the seeds or continue to let the extract infuse for up to one year.

VANILLA SUGAR

MAKES 4 CUPS (800G)

This simple vanilla sugar can be substituted for granulated sugar in any recipe that might benefit from a bit of additional vanilla flavor. It also makes a lovely gift, packaged in a jar with a nice label. As you use the vanilla-infused sugar, top off the jar with fresh sugar and the pods of spent vanilla beans. Spent vanilla beans are vanilla beans that have been used one time, to make ice cream, for example, but that still have a lot of vanilla flavor and are perfect for this use.

4 cups (800g) sugar

2 vanilla beans

Two 1-pint (480ml) jars or one 1-quart (1L) jar

Use the tip of a knife to slice each vanilla bean in half lengthwise and scrape out the seeds. Combine the vanilla seeds and sugar in a bowl and use your fingertips to work the vanilla seeds evenly into the sugar. Divide the scented sugar into the jars, along with the vanilla bean pods. Use the sugar immediately or store in a cool, dark place until ready to use.

SEASONAL LARDER

These are the seasonal items that complement the Year-Round Essentials. Some are preserves that I make every year and that last for months in the fridge or freezer, like Preserved Lemons (page 237) or Roasted Winter Squash Puree (page 238), and some are a bit more specific, like my favorite Spiced Rhubarb Compote (page 240) that I use to top everything from yogurt to toast.

POACHED QUINCE

MAKES 5 QUINCE

Hard, tannic quince must be poached into sweet submission before they can be included in cakes, pies, and tarts. Store leftover poached quince in their syrup in the refrigerator for up to one week. Be sure to save the syrup to use in cocktails or mix with seltzer for a refreshing quince soda.

5 medium quince (about 900g)

5 cups (1200ml) water

2 cups (400g) sugar

2 strips orange zest, peeled with a vegetable peeler

½ vanilla bean, split lengthwise to expose the seeds

½ lemon, juice and zest

Combine the water, sugar, orange zest, and vanilla bean in a medium saucepan; zest the lemon half into the pan, then squeeze in the juice. Bring to a simmer over medium heat.

While the mixture is heating, peel, core, and cut the quince into quarters. Be careful when handling the quince, as they are very firm and can be difficult to cut. Place them into the poaching liquid as you go to prevent oxidation. Top the pot off with additional water to cover the quince completely, if necessary.

Simmer the quince until tender, 30 to 40 minutes depending on the variety and freshness of the fruit. Your kitchen will smell heavenly.

Let the quince cool in their syrup until ready to use. They'll keep in the fridge for about a week.

PRESERVED LEMONS

MAKES 1 QUART (1L)

Making preserved lemons is one of my favorite winter canning projects and it's one of the easiest too. Meyer lemons are wonderful preserved because of their thin skins and small amount of bitter white pith, but regular lemons are also great. You'll be consuming the entire fruit, so use organic lemons if possible. This is really more of a formula than a specific recipe, so feel free to scale these amounts up or down depending on how many lemons you think you'll use.

8 to 10 organic lemons, well scrubbed

Kosher salt or coarse sea salt

Lemon juice, as needed

1 quart (1L) canning jar

CONTINUED

Slice the top and bottom off of each lemon. Stand the lemons up on one end and cut an "X" into each, stopping about ½ inch from the bottom so all four quarters are still connected at the base. Hold each lemon open with your fingertips and sprinkle a generous amount salt on the inside and outside of each one.

Cover the bottom of a the jar with a ¼-inch layer of salt and place the lemons in the jar one at a time, pressing down gently to release the juices. Fill the jar with lemons, leaving about 1 inch of headspace. If the lemons are not completely submerged in juice, top the jar off with additional lemon juice until they are covered. Sprinkle 2 tablespoons of salt over the top, screw on the lid, and give the jar a shake.

Let the jar sit at room temperature for three days, turning the jar upside down each day to distribute the salt and juices. After three days, store the jar in the refrigerator, making sure to turn it every couple of days. The lemons are ready when their rinds are very soft, about three weeks. To cook with the lemons, remove them from the jar and rinse with cool water. For some preparations, you'll use the pulp and rind; for others, you will remove and discard the pulp and seeds and just use the rind. Preserved lemons will keep in the fridge, submerged in juice, for one year.

ROASTED WINTER SQUASH PUREE

A 1¼-POUND (560G) SQUASH WILL YIELD ABOUT 2 CUPS (450G) OF PUREE

Use this method to roast any hard winter squash: butternut, red kuri, and kabocha all make a smooth and sweet puree.

Whole winter squash

Olive oil or vegetable oil

Position a rack in the center of the oven and preheat to 375ºF (190ºC). Use a sharp knife to slice off a thin piece of the bottom of the squash to give it a more stable base, then cut the squash in half from root to tip. Rub each half of the cut squash with olive oil or vegetable oil and place it cut side down on a baking sheet. Add a couple of tablespoons of water to the baking sheet. Bake until the squash feels soft and a fork slides all of the way through easily, 40 to 60 minutes, depending on the size of the squash. Let the squash sit on the baking sheet until it is cool enough to handle, then turn it over and use a spoon to scoop out the seeds. Discard the seeds and scoop out the flesh. Puree the flesh in a blender or food processor until smooth. Set the puree in a fine-mesh strainer set over a bowl for 30 minutes to drain excess liquid. Store the puree in an airtight container in the refrigerator for up to five days or in the freezer for up to three months.

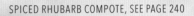

SPICED RHUBARB COMPOTE, SEE PAGE 240

SPICED RHUBARB COMPOTE

MAKES ABOUT 3 CUPS (675G)

This gently spiced compote can be stirred into oatmeal, dolloped on plain yogurt, or spread on buttery biscuits or croissants. It also makes a wonderful garnish for Rhubarb Semifreddo (page 24). Or just eat it with a spoon, as I often do. This recipe yields just a few small jars, so I don't usually go through the trouble of processing it in a water bath for shelf stability. Use the brightest, reddest rhubarb stalks you can find for this recipe, as they will create the most beautiful compote.

1 pound (450g) rhubarb stalks, leaves removed

2-inch (5cm) piece of fresh ginger, peeled and grated finely

½ vanilla bean

1¼ cups (250g) sugar

1 whole star anise

Juice of 1 lemon (about 3 tablespoons)

Chop the rhubarb into ½-inch pieces and place them in a nonreactive saucepan. Use the tip of a knife to split the vanilla bean lengthwise and scrape out the seeds. Add the sugar, grated ginger, star anise, vanilla seeds and pod, and lemon juice to the pan. Stir to combine, cover with a clean kitchen towel or plastic wrap, and let the mixture rest for 2 hours at room temperature. After a bit of rest the rhubarb should be nice and juicy.

Bring the mixture to a boil over high heat and cook, stirring occasionally with a rubber spatula, until thickened and jammy, 10 to 15 minutes.

Remove the star anise and vanilla pod; rinse off the vanilla pod and save it for another use. Transfer the compote to clean jars and store in the refrigerator for up to one month.

UNSWEETENED CRANBERRY JUICE

MAKES ABOUT 1 CUP (240ML)

Unsweetened cranberry juice is available at most health food stores, but it's easy to make at home with just cranberries and a bit of water—no juicer required.

1¼ cups (140g) fresh or frozen cranberries

¾ cup (180ml) water

Combine the cranberries and water in a saucepan. Cook over medium heat until the cranberries are soft and their skins have burst, about 10 minutes. Pour the mixture into a fine-mesh sieve lined with cheesecloth and press gently to extract all of the juice from the cranberries. Discard the solids. Store the juice in the refrigerator in an airtight container for up to one week or in an airtight container in the freezer for up to three months.

SOURCES

Find local farmers' markets
(www.localharvest.org)

Find local pick-your-own-fruit farms
(www.pickyourown.org)

Arrowhead Mills (www.arrowheadmills.com;
800-434-4246): flours

Beanilla (www.beanilla.com; 888-261-3384):
vanilla beans

Bob's Red Mill (www.bobsredmill.com;
800-349-2173): flours and specialty baking
ingredients

Kalustyan's (www.kalustyans.com;
800-352-3451): Middle Eastern specialty
ingredients and spices

King Arthur Flour (www.kingarthurflour.com;
800-827-6836): flours, Lyle's Golden Syrup,
specialty baking ingredients, and baking pans

Nuts.com (www.nuts.com; 800-558-6887):
bee pollen, cacao nibs, dates, dried fruit, flours,
and nuts

Penzey's (www.penzeys.com; 800-741-7787):
spices and vanilla beans

ABOUT THE AUTHOR

YOSSY AREFI is a food photographer and the creator of the award-winning blog *Apt. 2B Baking Co.* She writes a regular column for Food52 and her work has been featured in *Bon Appétit, Saveur, Good Housekeeping, Modern Farmer, T Magazine,* and more.

She lives in Brooklyn, New York.

PHOTO BY CHRISTINE HAN

ACKNOWLEDGMENTS

I feel so fortunate to have been able to make this book with the talented team at Ten Speed. Thank you to Ali Slagle for encouraging me to take on this project. Thank you to Jenny Wapner, Clara Sankey, and Ashley Lima for shaping this book so beautifully, and for answering my innumerable questions along the way. Ashley, I am so thrilled with your gorgeous design. Thank you to the marketing and publicity team, Erin Welke and Ashley Matuszak for believing in this book. To everyone else who worked on this book whose names I do not know, thank you.

Pete, this would not have been possible without you. Thank you for your patience and unwavering support during this process, and always.

Many thanks to my dear family whose love for food and gardening is an inspiration. Thanks mom and dad for sending me boxes full of treats from your garden every year. They make Brooklyn feel like home.

Jim, thank you so much for your thoughtful guidance.

Thank you to the Scoville family for opening your home to me and this project.

Thank you to the Storch family touring me around your little slice of the world.

Julia Gartland and Shae Irving, thank you. The winter chapter would be a lot less sunny without you.

Many thanks to the USDA National Clonal Germplasm Repository in Corvallis for sharing a small piece of your incredible collection with me. Thank you to the farmers at Radke's Bluberries, Gathering Together Farm, Fishkill Farms, Lawrence Farm Orchards, and the many farmers at the Union Square Farmers' Market.

To Mud Australia and Clair Catillaz of Clam Lab thank you for entrusting me with so many of your incredible ceramics. Rachel, thank you for letting me raid your silverware drawer.

To my pal Danielle, thank you for your inspiration and keen eye.

Thank you to all of the recipe testers who took time to bake from this book generously and enthusiastically.

To the readers and supporters of *Apt. 2B Baking Co.*, thank you.

INDEX

A

Almonds
    Citrus Almond Thumbprints
      with Summer Jam, 219
    Crisp Topping (variation), 230
    Currant and Gooseberry
      Buckle, 76–78
Apples, 145
    Blueberry Skillet Cobbler
      with Whole Wheat Biscuits
      (variation), 72
    Campfire Crisp, 155
    Caramelized Apple Fritters, 151–53
    Concord Grape and Plum
      Butter, 132
    Concord Grape Pie with Rye
      Crust, 128–31
    Marie-Danielle's Apple Tart, 146
    Spelt Shortcakes with Roasted
      Stone Fruit (variation), 103
Apricots, 63
    Apricot and Berry Galette with
      Saffron Sugar, 64
    Roasted Apricot and Buttermilk
      Sherbet, 68
    The Simplest Strawberry Tart
      (variation), 36
    Small-Batch Apricot Jam, 67
    Spelt Shortcakes with Roasted
      Stone Fruit, 100–103

B

Bars
    Nectarine and Blackberry
      Pie Bars, 96
    Rangpur Lime Bars with
      Saffron, 215
Berries, 71
    Apricot and Berry Galette
      with Saffron Sugar, 64
    Black Fruit Tart, 85
    Cherry and Poppy Seed
      Yogurt Cake (variation), 59
    Coconut Cream Fool with
      Raspberries (variation), 108
    Spelt Shortcakes with Roasted
      Stone Fruit (variation), 103
    See also individual berries
Blackberries
    Apricot and Berry Galette with
      Saffron Sugar, 64

Blackberry and Sage Cream
    Puffs, 81–82
Black Fruit Tart, 85
Coconut Cream Fool with
    Raspberries (variation), 108
Cranberry Bread Pudding
    (variation), 186
Currant and Gooseberry Buckle
    (variation), 78
Nectarine and Blackberry Pie
    Bars, 96
The Simplest Strawberry Tart
    (variation), 36
Blondies, Browned-Butter Date, 225
Blueberries
    Apricot and Berry Galette with
      Saffron Sugar, 64
    Black Fruit Tart, 85
    Blueberry Skillet Cobbler with
      Whole Wheat Biscuits, 72
    Cranberry Bread Pudding
      (variation), 186
    Crème Fraîche and Blueberry
      Ice Cream, 75
    Currant and Gooseberry Buckle
      (variation), 78
Bread Pudding, Cranberry, 186
Buckle, Currant and Gooseberry, 76–78
Buckwheat flour, 227
    Black Fruit Tart, 85
    Buckwheat Tart Shell, 233–34
    Cacao Nib Poppy Seed
      Wafers, 39–40
Buttercream, Raspberry, 112

C

Cacao nibs
    Cacao Nib Poppy Seed
      Wafers, 39–40
    Fresh Mint Ice Cream with
      Cacao Nibs, 14
Cakes
    Butternut Squash Tea Cake, 174
    Cherry and Poppy Seed
      Yogurt Cake, 59
    Chocolate Celebration Cake
      with Fresh Raspberry
      Buttercream, 111–13
    Cornmeal and Ricotta Cake
      with Cranberries, 189

Ginger Quince Upside-Down
    Cake, 166–69
Grapefruit and Meyer Lemon
    Bundt Cake, 208–11
Lemon Verbena Olive Oil Cake, 16
A Pear-Packed Chestnut Cake, 158
Pistachio Pound Cake with
    Strawberries in Lavender
    Sugar, 43–44
Rhubarb and Rye Upside-Down
    Cake, 31–32
Soft Chocolate and Fig Cake, 123
Sticky Toffee Pudding with
    Cranberries, 222
Campari and Strawberry Paletas, 47
Cantaloupe and Mint Yogurt Pops, 88
Caramel
    Caramel-Swirled Roasted Squash
      Ice Cream, 179
    Crème Fraîche Caramel Sauce, 229
    Salty Caramel Sauce, 229
Chamomile Honey Panna Cotta, 12
Cherries, 49
    Browned-Butter Date Blondies, 225
    Cherry and Chocolate
      Turnovers, 50
    Cherry and Poppy Seed
      Yogurt Cake, 59
    Cherry and Rhubarb Slab Pie, 53–54
    Currant and Gooseberry Buckle
      (variation), 78
    Spelt Shortcakes with Roasted
      Stone Fruit, 100–103
    Spiked Cherry Sorbet, 55
Chestnut Cake, A Pear-Packed, 158
Chocolate
    Browned-Butter Date Blondies, 225
    Cherry and Chocolate
      Turnovers, 50
    Chocolate Celebration Cake
      with Fresh Raspberry
      Buttercream, 111–13
    Chocolate Sesame Tart with
      Grapefruit, 194
    Chocolate Tart Shell, 234–35
    Soft Chocolate and Fig Cake, 123
    See also Cacao nibs
Citrus fruit, 193
    Citrus Almond Thumbprints
      with Summer Jam, 219
    See also individual fruits

Cobbler, Blueberry Skillet, with
    Whole Wheat Biscuits, 72
Coconut Cream Fool with
    Raspberries, 108
Compote, Spiced Rhubarb, 240
Cookies
    Cacao Nib Poppy Seed
        Wafer, 39–40
    Citrus Almond Thumbprints
        with Summer Jam, 219
    Cornmeal and Ricotta Cake
        with Cranberries, 189
Cranberries, 185
    Blueberry Skillet Cobbler with
        Whole Wheat Biscuits
        (variation), 72
    Campfire Crisp (variation), 155
    Cornmeal and Ricotta Cake
        with Cranberries, 189
    Cranberry and Pear
        Pandowdy, 190
    Cranberry Bread Pudding, 186
    Currant and Gooseberry Buckle
        (variation), 78
    Jeweled Pavlovas with
        Cranberry Curd, 138–41
    Sticky Toffee Pudding with
        Cranberries, 222
    Unsweetened Cranberry Juice, 240
Cream Puffs, Blackberry and
    Sage, 81–82
Crème Fraîche, 229
    Crème Fraîche and Blueberry
        Ice Cream, 75
    Crème Fraîche Caramel Sauce, 229
Crisps
    Campfire Crisp, 155
    Crisp Topping, 230
Currants
    Coconut Cream Fool with
        Raspberries (variation), 108
    Currant and Gooseberry
        Buckle, 76–78

D

Dates, 221
    Browned-Butter Date Blondies, 225
    Sticky Toffee Pudding with
        Cranberries, 222
Donuts, Blood Orange
    Old-Fashioned, 197–98

F

Figs, 119
    Black Fruit Tart, 85
    Soft Chocolate and Fig Cake, 123
    Wine-Roasted Figs with Whipped
        Honeyed Ricotta, 120
Flours
    buying and storing, 227
    types of, 227
    See also individual flours
Fool, Coconut Cream, with
    Raspberries, 108
Fritters, Caramelized Apple, 151–53
Fruit preserves
    Concord Grape and Plum
        Butter, 132
    Quick Marmalade with Blood
        Oranges and Meyer
        Lemons, 201–2
    Small-Batch Apricot Jam, 67

G

Galettes
    Apricot and Berry Galette with
        Saffron Sugar, 64
    Rhubarb and Rose Galettes, 20–23
Ginger
    Ginger Quince Upside-Down
        Cake, 166–69
    Gingery Lime Posset, 216
    Persimmon Sorbet with
        Ginger and Vanilla, 142
Gingersnap Crust, 205
Gooseberry and Currant
    Buckle, 76–78
Granita, Watermelon, with
    Chile and Lime, 91
Grapefruit
    Chocolate Sesame Tart with
        Grapefruit, 194
    Grapefruit and Meyer Lemon
        Bundt Cake, 208–11
Grapes, 127
    Black Fruit Tart, 85
    Campfire Crisp, 155
    Concord Grape and Plum
        Butter, 132
    Concord Grape Pie with
        Rye Crust, 128–31

H

Hazelnuts
    Citrus Almond Thumbprints with
        Summer Jam (variation), 219
    Crisp Topping (variation), 230
    Plum Pie with Hazelnut
        Crumb, 104

I

Ice cream
    Caramel-Swirled Roasted Squash
        Ice Cream, 179
    Crème Fraîche and Blueberry
        Ice Cream, 75
    Fresh Mint Ice Cream with
        Cacao Nibs, 14
    Preserved Lemon Ice Cream, 212
    Strawberry Ice Cream
        Sandwiches with Cacao Nib
        Poppy Seed Wafers, 39–40

J

Jam, Small-Batch Apricot, 67

L

Lemons
    Cherry and Poppy Seed
        Yogurt Cake (variation), 59
    Grapefruit and Meyer Lemon
        Bundt Cake, 208–11
    Preserved Lemon Ice Cream, 212
    Preserved Lemons, 237–38
    Quick Marmalade with
        Blood Oranges and Meyer
        Lemons, 201–2
Lemon verbena
    Lemon Verbena Olive Oil Cake, 16
    Wine-Soaked Peaches with
        Lemon Verbena, 99
Limes
    Cherry and Poppy Seed
        Yogurt Cake, 59
    Gingery Lime Posset, 216
    Rangpur Lime Bars with
        Saffron, 215
    Watermelon Granita with
        Chile and Lime, 91

M

Marie-Danielle's Apple Tart, 146
Marmalade, Quick, with Blood
    Oranges and Meyer
    Lemons, 201–2

Mascarpone
   Black Fruit Tart, 85
   The Simplest Strawberry Tart, 36
Melons, 87
   Cantaloupe and Mint Yogurt
     Pops, 88
   Watermelon Granita with
     Chile and Lime, 91
Mint
   Cantaloupe and Mint Yogurt
     Pops, 88
   Fresh Mint Ice Cream with
     Cacao Nibs, 14

N

Nectarines, 95
   Cherry and Poppy Seed
     Yogurt Cake (variation), 59
   Nectarine and Blackberry
     Pie Bars, 96
   The Simplest Strawberry Tart
     (variation), 36
   Spelt Shortcakes with Roasted
     Stone Fruit, 100–103

O

Oats
   Cacao Nib Poppy Seed
     Wafers, 39–40
   Crisp Topping, 230
Oranges
   Blood Orange Old-Fashioned
     Donuts, 197–98
   Quick Marmalade with
     Blood Oranges and Meyer
     Lemons, 201–2

P

Paletas, Strawberry and Campari, 47
Pandowdy, Cranberry and Pear, 190
Panna Cotta, Chamomile Honey, 12
Pastry Cream, 230–31
Pavlovas
   Jeweled Pavlovas with Cranberry
     Curd, 138–41
   Roasted Rhubarb Pavlova, 27–28
Peaches, 95
   Cherry and Poppy Seed Yogurt
     Cake (variation), 59
   Cranberry Bread Pudding
     (variation), 186
   The Simplest Strawberry Tart
     (variation), 36

Spelt Shortcakes with Roasted
   Stone Fruit, 100–103
Wine-Soaked Peaches with
   Lemon Verbena, 99
Pears, 157
   Blueberry Skillet Cobbler with
     Whole Wheat Biscuits
     (variation), 72
   Cranberry and Pear Pandowdy, 190
   A Pear-Packed Chestnut Cake, 158
   Pear Pie with Crème Fraîche
     Caramel, 161–62
   Spelt Shortcakes with Roasted
     Stone Fruit (variation), 103
Pecans
   Butternut Squash Tea Cake, 174
   Crisp Topping (variation), 230
Persimmons, 137
   Jeweled Pavlovas with Cranberry
     Curd, 138–41
   Persimmon Sorbet with Ginger
     and Vanilla, 142
Pie crusts
   All-Butter Pie Crust, 228
   Gingersnap Crust, 205
   Rye Pie Crust, 228
   Spelt Pie Crust, 228
Pies
   Cherry and Rhubarb Slab Pie, 53–54
   Concord Grape Pie with
     Rye Crust, 128–31
   Pear Pie with Crème Fraîche
     Caramel, 161–62
   Plum Pie with Hazelnut
     Crumb, 104
   Tangerine Cream Pie, 205–6
   Winter Luxury Pumpkin Pie, 180
Pistachios
   Chamomile Honey Panna Cotta, 12
   Pistachio Pound Cake with
     Strawberries in Lavender
     Sugar, 43–44
   Quince and Pistachio Frangipane
     Tartlets, 170
   Rhubarb Semifreddo, 24
Plums, 95
   Black Fruit Tart, 85
   Campfire Crisp, 155
   Cherry and Poppy Seed
     Yogurt Cake (variation), 59
   Concord Grape and Plum
     Butter, 132
   Plum Pie with Hazelnut
     Crumb, 104

Spelt Shortcakes with Roasted
   Stone Fruit, 100–103
Pomegranates, 137
   Jeweled Pavlovas with Cranberry
     Curd, 138–41
Pops
   Cantaloupe and Mint Yogurt
     Pops, 88
   Strawberry and Campari
     Paletas, 47
Posset, Gingery Lime, 216
Puddings
   Cranberry Bread Pudding, 186
   Sticky Toffee Pudding with
     Cranberries, 222
Puff pastry
   Cherry and Chocolate
     Turnovers, 50
   Marie-Danielle's Apple Tarte, 146
   Spelt Quick Puff Pastry, 231–32
Pumpkin, 173
   Caramel-Swirled Roasted Squash
     Ice Cream, 179
   Winter Luxury Pumpkin Pie, 180
Pumpkin seeds
   Butternut Squash Tea Cake, 174

Q

Quince, 165
   Ginger Quince Upside-Down
     Cake, 166–69
   Poached Quince, 237
   Quince and Pistachio Frangipane
     Tartlets, 170

R

Raspberries, 107
   Black Fruit Tart, 85
   Chocolate Celebration Cake
     with Fresh Raspberry
     Buttercream, 111–13
   Coconut Cream Fool with
     Raspberries, 108
   Cranberry Bread Pudding
     (variation), 186
   Raspberry Sorbet with Pink
     Peppercorns, 116
   The Simplest Strawberry Tart
     (variation), 36
Rhubarb, 19
   Blueberry Skillet Cobbler with
     Whole Wheat Biscuits
     (variation), 72

Cherry and Rhubarb Slab Pie, 53–54
Coconut Cream Fool with
    Raspberries (variation), 108
Rhubarb and Rose Galettes, 20–23
Rhubarb and Rye Upside-Down
    Cake, 31–32
Rhubarb Semifreddo, 24
Roasted Rhubarb Pavlova, 27–28
Spelt Shortcakes with Roasted
    Stone Fruit (variation), 103
Spiced Rhubarb Compote, 240
Ricotta
    Cornmeal and Ricotta Cake
        with Cranberries, 189
    Wine-Roasted Figs with Whipped
        Honeyed Ricotta, 120
Rose Cream, 20, 23
Rye flour, 227
    Apricot and Berry Galette
        with Saffron Sugar, 64
    Blackberry and Sage Cream
        Puffs, 81–82
    Concord Grape Pie with Rye
        Crust, 128–31
    Cranberry and Pear Pandowdy, 190
    Crisp Topping (variation), 230
    Plum Pie with Hazelnut
        Crumb, 104
    Rhubarb and Rye Upside-Down
        Cake, 31–32
    Rye Pie Crust, 228
    The Simplest Strawberry Tart, 36

S
Sauces
    Brandied Toffee Sauce, 222
    Crème Fraîche Caramel Sauce, 229
    Salty Caramel Sauce, 229
Semifreddo, Rhubarb, 24
Sherbet, Roasted Apricot and
    Buttermilk, 68
Shortcakes, Spelt, with Roasted
    Stone Fruits, 100–103
Sorbet
    Persimmon Sorbet with Ginger
        and Vanilla, 142
    Raspberry Sorbet with Pink
        Peppercorns, 116
    Spiked Cherry Sorbet, 55
Spelt flour, 227
    Cherry and Chocolate
        Turnovers, 50
    Cranberry and Pear Pandowdy, 190

Marie-Danielle's Apple Tarte, 146
Rhubarb and Rose Galettes, 20–23
Spelt Pie Crust, 228
Spelt Quick Puff Pastry, 231–32
Spelt Shortcakes with Roasted
    Stone Fruit, 100–103
Squash, 173
    Butternut Squash Tea Cake, 174
    Caramel-Swirled Roasted Squash
        Ice Cream, 179
    Roasted Winter Squash Puree, 238
Sticky Toffee Pudding with
    Cranberries, 222
Stone fruits, 95
    Cherry and Poppy Seed Yogurt
        Cake (variation), 59
    Spelt Shortcakes with Roasted
        Stone Fruit, 100–103
    See also individual fruits
Strawberries, 35
    Blueberry Skillet Cobbler with
        Whole Wheat Biscuits
        (variation), 72
    Pistachio Pound Cake with
        Strawberries in Lavender
        Sugar, 43–44
    The Simplest Strawberry Tart, 36
    Strawberry and Campari
        Paletas, 47
    Strawberry Ice Cream
        Sandwiches with Cacao Nib
        Poppy Seed Wafers, 39–40
Sugar, Vanilla, 235, 237

T
Tangerine Cream Pie, 205–6
Tarts and tartlets
    Apricot and Berry Galette with
        Saffron Sugar, 64
    Black Fruit Tart, 85
    Chocolate Sesame Tart with
        Grapefruit, 194
    Marie-Danielle's Apple Tart, 146
    Quince and Pistachio Frangipane
        Tartlets, 170
    Rhubarb and Rose Galettes, 20–23
    The Simplest Strawberry Tart, 36
Tart shells
    All-Purpose Tart Shell, 232–33
    Buckwheat Tart Shell, 233–34
    Chocolate Tart Shell, 234–35
Tea Cake, Butternut Squash, 174
Turnovers, Cherry and Chocolate, 50

V
Vanilla
    Vanilla Extract, 235
    Vanilla Sugar, 235, 237

W
Walnuts
    Browned-Butter Date Blondies, 225
    Butternut Squash Tea Cake, 174
    Citrus Almond Thumbprints
        with Summer Jam
        (variation), 219
    Crisp Topping (variation), 230
    A Pear-Packed Chestnut Cake, 158
Watermelon Granita with Chile
    and Lime, 91
Whole wheat flour, 227
    Blueberry Skillet Cobbler with
        Whole Wheat Biscuits, 72
    Butternut Squash Tea Cake, 174
    Campfire Crisp, 155
    Crisp Topping (variation), 230
    Nectarine and Blackberry Pie
        Bars, 96
Wine
    Wine-Roasted Figs with Whipped
        Honeyed Ricotta, 120
    Wine-Soaked Peaches with
        Lemon Verbena, 99
Winter Luxury Pumpkin Pie, 180

Y
Yogurt
    Cantaloupe and Mint Yogurt
        Pops, 88
    Cherry and Poppy Seed Yogurt
        Cake, 59

Published in the United States by Ten Speed Press, an imprint of the Crown
Publishing Group, a division of Penguin Random House LLC, New York.
www.crownpublishing.com
www.tenspeed.com

Ten Speed Press and the Ten Speed Press colophon are registered
trademarks of Penguin Random House LLC.

A handful of the recipes in this work were inspired by ones which originally
appeared on Yossy Arefi's website: apt2bbaKingco.com.

Library of Congress Cataloging-in-Publication Data
Arefi, Yossy, author.
  Sweeter off the vine : fruit desserts for every season / Yossy Arefi.
      pages cm
  Summary: "A cozy collection of heirloom-quality recipes for pies, cakes, tarts,
ice cream, preserves, and other sweet treats that cherishes the fruit of every
season"— Provided by publisher.
  Includes bibliographical references and index.
1. Cooking (Fruit) 2. Desserts. 3. Seasonal cooking. I. Title.
  TX811.A74 2016
  641.6′4—dc23
                              2015032318

Hardcover ISBN: 978-1-60774-858-8
eBook ISBN: 978-1-60774-859-5

Printed in China

Design by Ashley Lima

10 9 8 7 6 5 4 3 2 1

First Edition

METRIC CONVERSION CHARTS

1 inch = 2.5cm
16 ounces = 1 pound = 450g
1 cup = 8 fluid ounces = 240ml

OVEN TEMPERATURE CONVERSIONS
Gas mark $1/4$ = 225°F = 110°C
Gas mark $1/2$ = 250°F = 130°C
Gas mark 1 = 275°F = 140°C
Gas mark 2 = 300°F = 150°C
Gas mark 3 = 325°F = 170°C
Gas mark 4 = 350°F = 180°C
Gas mark 5 = 375°F = 190°C
Gas mark 6 = 400°F = 200°C
Gas mark 7 = 425°F = 220°C

METRIC EQUIVALENTS
1 cup all purpose flour = 125g
1 cup cake flour, unsifted = 120g
1 cup buckwheat flour = 140g
1 cup rye flour = 130g
1 cup spelt flour = 130g
1 cup whole wheat flour = 130g
1 cup cocoa powder, unsifted = 100g
1 cup cornmeal = 150g
1 cup old fashioned oats = 90g
1 cup confectioner's sugar, unsifted = 120g
1 cup granulated sugar = 200g
1 cup brown sugar, packed = 200g
1 cup pecans = 100g
1 cup pepitas (pumpkin seeds) = 130g
1 cup shelled pistachios = 130g
1 cup sliced almonds = 100g
1 cup whole almonds = 140g
1 cup walnuts = 100g
1 cup chopped chocolate = 170g
1 cup honey = 240ml
1 cup butter = 225g
1 stick butter = 115g
1 cup crème fraiche = 225g
1 cup mascarpone = 225g
1 cup ricotta = 235g
1 cup sour cream = 225g
1 cup yogurt = 225g